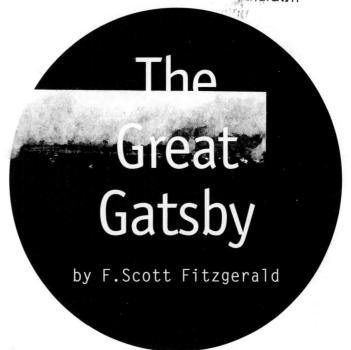

The Great Gatsby

by F. Scott Fitzgerald

Anne Crow

Series Editors:
Nicola Onyett and Luke McBratney

HODDER
EDUCATION
AN HACHETTE UK COMPANY

The publisher would like to thank the following for permission to reproduce copyright material:

Acknowledgements:

pp.vi, 13, 19, 30, 36, 40, 43, 72: F. Scott Fitzgerald: from *A Life in Letters*, ed. Matthew J. Bruccoli (Scribner, 1995); **p.13: A.E. Dyson:** from 'Modern Fiction Studies VII' (Purdue University, Lafayette, Indiana, 1961); **pp.13, 15, 29, 30, 36, 37, 38, 43, 44, 47, 50, 50–1, 52, 56, 57, 58, 59, 69, 101–4: F. Scott Fitzgerald:** from *The Great Gatsby* (Scribner, 2004), reprinted with the permission of Scribner, a division of Simon & Schuster, Inc. from THE GREAT GATSBY by F. Scott Fitzgerald. Copyright © 1929 by Curtis Publishing Co.. All rights reserved; **pp.21, 76: William Troy:** from 'Fitzgerald – the Authority of Failure' from *Accent* (Accent, 1945); **p.27: Roger Lewis:** from 'Money, Love and Aspiration in *The Great Gatsby*' from *New Essays on the Great Gatsby*, ed. Matthew J. Bruccoli (Cambridge University Press, 1985); **p.30: Arthur Mizener:** from *F. Scott Fitzgerald: A Collection of Critical Essays (Twentieth Century Views)* (Prentice Hall, 1963); **p.32: W.M. Thackeray:** from *Vanity Fair* (1848); **p.33: F. Scott Fitzgerald:** from 'Absolution' from *All the Sad Young Men* (1926); **p.37: C.W.E Bigsby:** from 'The Two Identities of F. Scott Fitzgerald' from *The American Novel in the Nineteen Twenties*, eds. Malcolm Bradbury and David Palmer (Arnold, 1971); **pp.39,77: Judith Fetterley:** from *The Resisting Reader: A Feminist Approach to American Fiction* (Indiana University Press, 1978), reproduced by permission of Indiana University Press; **pp.41, 77: Lionel Trilling:** from *The Liberal Imagination* (New York Review Books Classics, 2008); **p.48: James E. Miller Jr.:** from *The Fictional Technique of F. Scott Fizgerald* (New York University Press, 1964); **pp.50, 75: Joseph Conrad:** from *The Nigger of the Narcissus* (1897); **pp.50, 63: Andrew Turnbull:** from *Scott Fitzgerald* (Vintage, 2004), reproduced by permission of David Higham Associates Ltd.; **p.64: F.S. Fitzgerald:** from 'My Lost City' from *The Crack-Up* (New Directions, 2009), by F. Scott Fitzgerald, from THE CRACK-UP, copyright ©1945 by New Directions Publishing Corp. Reprinted by permission of New Directions Publishing Corp; **p.65: F. Scott Fitzgerald:** from 'The Swimmers' from *The Short Stories of F. Scott Fitzgerald* (Scribner, 1995); **p.66: Emma Lazarus:** from 'The New Colossus' (1883); **p.67: Marcus Cunliffe:** from *The Literature of the United States* (Penguin, 1986); **p.72: Henry Dan Piper:** from *The Great Gatsby: The Novel, The Critics, The Background* (Longman, 1970); **p.76: H.L. Mencken:** from an article, published in *The Baltimore Evening Sun* (The Baltimore Evening Sun, May 1925); **p.76: Isabel Paterson:** taken from an article, published in *The New York Herald Tribune* (The New York Herald Tribune, 19th April 1925); **p.77: Arthur Mizener:** from 'F. Scott Fitzgerald 1896–1940: The Poet of Borrowed Time', from *Lives of Eighteen from Princeton* (Princeton University Press, 1946); **p.77: R.W. Stallman:** from 'Gatsby and the Hole in Time' from *Modern Fiction Studies, vol. 1, no. 4* (Purdue University, Lafayette, Indiana, 1961); **p.99: F. Scott Fitzgerald:** adapted from *The Great Gatsby* (Scribner, 2004), reprinted with the permission of Scribner, a division of Simon & Schuster, Inc. from THE GREAT GATSBY by F. Scott Fitzgerald. Copyright © 1929 by Curtis Publishing Co. All rights reserved.

Every effort has been made to trace or contact all copyright holders, but if any have been inadvertently overlooked the Publishers will be pleased to make the necessary arrangements at the first opportunity.

Photo credits:

p.12 © johnandersonphoto - iStock via Thinkstock/Getty Images; **p.17** public domain; **p.22** © Fine Art Images/Heritage Images/Getty Images; **p.32** © BAZMARK FILMS / THE KOBAL COLLECTION; **p.34** Public domain; **p.35** © PARAMOUNT / THE KOBAL COLLECTION; **p.36** © PARAMOUNT / THE KOBAL COLLECTION; **p.39** Moviestore Collection/REX; **p.55** © AF archive / Alamy; **p.65** © Pictorial Press Ltd / Alamy; **p.66** © Public domain; **p.71** © c.Warner Br/Everett/REX

Although every effort has been made to ensure that website addresses are correct at time of going to press, Hodder Education cannot be held responsible for the content of any website mentioned. It is sometimes possible to find a relocated web page by typing in the address of the home page for a website in the URL window of your browser.

Orders: please contact Bookpoint Ltd, 130 Milton Park, Abingdon, Oxon OX14 4SB. Telephone: (44) 01235 827720. Fax: (44) 01235 400454. Lines are open 9.00–17.00, Monday to Saturday, with a 24-hour message answering service. Visit our website at www. hoddereducation.co.uk

First published in 2016 by

Hodder Education
An Hachette UK Company,
Carmelite House, 50 Victoria Embankment
London EC4Y 0DZ

Impression number	5	4	3	2	1
Year	2020	2019	2018	2017	2016

Cover photo (and throughout) © Marcus Lindstrom/istockphoto.com

Illustrations by Integra Software Services Pvt. Ltd. and Philip Allen

Typeset in 11/13pt Univers LT Std 47 Light Condensed by Integra Software Services Pvt. Ltd., Pondicherry, India

Printed in Italy

A catalogue record for this title is available from the British Library

ISBN 978-1-4718-5407-1

Contents

Why read this guide?

The purposes of this A-level Literature Guide are to enable you to organise your thoughts and responses to the text, deepen your understanding of key features and aspects and help you to address the particular requirements of examination questions and non-exam assessment tasks in order to obtain the best possible grade. It will also prove useful to those of you writing an NEA piece on the text as it provides a number of summaries, lists, analyses and references to help with the content and construction of the assignment.

Note that teachers and examiners are seeking above all else evidence of an *informed personal response to the text*. A guide such as this can help you to understand the text, form your own opinions, and suggest areas to think about, but it cannot replace your own ideas and responses as an informed and autonomous reader.

Page references in this guide refer to the Penguin Modern Classics edition of *The Great Gatsby* edited by Tony Tanner (2000). This edition has excellent introductory material and some notes. Where a publication is given in the **Taking it further** section on pages 105–6, the author's surname and publication date only are cited after the first full reference.

How to make the most of this guide

You may find it useful to read sections of this guide when you need them, rather than reading it from start to finish. For example, you may find it helpful to read the 'Contexts' section before you start reading the text, or to read the 'Chapter summaries and commentaries' section in conjunction with the text – whether to back up your first reading of it at school or college or to help you revise. The sections relating to the Assessment Objectives will be especially useful in the weeks leading up to the exam.

This guide is designed to help you to raise your achievement in your examination response to *The Great Gatsby*. It is intended for you to use throughout your AS/A-level English Literature course. It will help you when you are studying the novel for the first time and also during your revision.

The following features have been used throughout this guide to help you focus your understanding of the novel:

Context

Context boxes give contextual information that relates directly to particular aspects of the text.

Build critical skills

Broaden your thinking about the text by answering the questions in the **Build critical skills** boxes. These help you to consider your own opinions in order to develop your skills of criticism and analysis.

TASK

Tasks are short and focused. They allow you to engage directly with a particular aspect of the text.

Taking it further ▶▶

Taking it further boxes suggest and provide further background or illuminating parallels to the text.

CRITICAL VIEW

Critical view boxes highlight a particular critical viewpoint that is relevant to an aspect of the main text. This allows you to develop the higher-level skills needed to come up with your own interpretation of a text.

Top ten quotation

Top ten quotation

A cross-reference to Top ten quotations (see pages 101–104 of this guide), where each quotation is accompanied by a commentary that shows why it is important.

After the Great War, the veterans, relieved to have survived, wanted to forget their experiences; they turned their backs on their parents' values and were determined to have a good time. Fitzgerald dubbed the era 'The Jazz Age' and put music at the heart of this novel. After Gatsby's death, Nick 'could still hear the music' of Gatsby's parties. The surname of Fitzgerald's fictional composer, Tostoff, symbolises the contempt of the young for the old values and represents the decadent values of the Roaring Twenties. His supposed tune, 'Jazz History of the World', suggests that this generation ignored everything that happened before their own time; the world had been reborn after the war.

In this novel, first published in 1925, Fitzgerald captures the spirit of the hedonism of the age, but he also reveals the disillusionment associated with a break with traditions. His narrator's ingrained old-fashioned values lead him to despise the decadence, but, simultaneously, he is enchanted by the excitement and wishes he too could abandon his principles. Nick Carraway is partially involved in the story, and this makes him unreliable. His account is coloured by his feelings and prejudices; his romantic soul and vivid imagination lead him to draw conclusions which are not necessarily true.

Fitzgerald is able to weave a web of mystery around Gatsby because Nick does not experience all events first hand. Many important questions are left unanswered, and this makes it a fascinating novel to explore. Although the films are brilliant media for bringing the Roaring Twenties to life, they cannot preserve the mystery.

In Jack Clayton's film (1974), Gatsby is shot while standing at the edge of the pool. In Baz Luhrmann's film (2013), the air bed sinks when the bullets puncture it. In Robert Markowitz's film (2000), Wilson shoots Gatsby in the heart without the bullet puncturing the mattress. How much more satisfying to read Nick's account and wonder what really happened. His detailed description of the water's movement as the pool is emptied suggests that he cannot bear to look at the body, and so Fitzgerald has left the murder open to question. Was Gatsby actually shot on the mattress or placed on it afterwards? Was Wilson a crack shot or had somebody else shot Gatsby and then Wilson in order to implicate him?

At the inquest, Nick observes that Wilson was blamed 'in order that the case might remain in its simplest form'. Does this evasive wording suggest that the inquest came to the wrong conclusion deliberately? We shall never know, but we do know that every word Fitzgerald used was carefully chosen, and so the ambiguity is deliberate. He wanted Gatsby's death to be as mysterious as his life.

Nick Carraway introduces himself, telling his readers that he fought in the Great War, and this made him restlessly unwilling to work in the family business on his return. He moved from the Midwest of America to New York in the summer of 1922, to learn about the bond business. He rented a cheap bungalow in the West Egg district of Long Island, a wealthy but unfashionable area populated by the newly rich. Nick's next-door neighbour in West Egg is a mysterious man named Jay Gatsby, who lives in a huge mock-French mansion and throws extravagant parties every weekend.

Unlike other inhabitants of West Egg, Nick boasts a possible connection with the English aristocracy, was educated at Yale University and has social connections in East Egg, the fashionable area of Long Island where the established upper classes live. One evening, Nick drives to East Egg for dinner with his cousin, Daisy Buchanan, and her husband, Tom, whom Nick knew at Yale. Daisy and Tom introduce Nick to Daisy's friend, Jordan Baker, a young professional golfer, with whom he later begins a romantic relationship.

Nick learns that Tom has a lover, and, soon after this, Tom takes Nick to meet Myrtle Wilson, the wife of the garage mechanic in the valley of ashes, a grey industrial dumping ground between the Eggs and Manhattan. Nick travels to the city with Tom and Myrtle, and, at a vulgar party in the apartment Tom keeps for the affair, Myrtle taunts Tom about Daisy. Tom responds by breaking her nose, and Nick leaves hurriedly.

Nick is invited to one of Gatsby's legendary parties, where he once more meets Jordan Baker, who introduces him to Gatsby, a young man with an irresistible smile who speaks with an elaborate formality. He and Nick both served in the same division of the US army during the war, and they share a few vague reminiscences.

Another day, Gatsby takes Nick to New York in his gorgeous car and gives him an extravagantly fictitious account of his life. In a cellar restaurant, he introduces Nick to Meyer Wolfshiem, who supposedly fixed the Baseball World Series in 1919.

After lunch, Nick meets Jordan and learns that Gatsby knew Daisy in Louisville in 1917 and is deeply in love with her. He spends many nights staring at the green light at the end of her dock, across the bay from his mansion. Gatsby's extravagant lifestyle is simply an attempt to attract Daisy. Nick is overwhelmed by the splendour of Gatsby's dream. Jordan then tells Nick that Gatsby wants him to arrange a meeting with Daisy. Nick invites Daisy to tea, warning her not to bring Tom, but not telling her that Gatsby will also be there. After an initially awkward reunion, Gatsby and Daisy revive their relationship and begin an affair. However, Gatsby wants more than an affair; he hopes that they can pick up the

Context

Frances Scott Fitzgerald and his wife, Zelda, lived in Great Neck, Long Island, while he was planning *The Great Gatsby*.

Context

Fitzgerald enlisted in May, 1917, but he did not complete his training and so he did not go to the war. See **Contexts** on page 63.

relationship from the point when he went to war, and that Daisy will leave Tom and her daughter.

During the summer, Tom grows increasingly suspicious of his wife's relationship with Gatsby. At a luncheon party, Daisy behaves indiscreetly, and Tom realises they are in love. Tom is outraged. Daisy suggests they go to town, and Tom demands to drive Gatsby's car. Daisy chooses to travel with Gatsby in Tom's car. Tom stops in the valley of ashes for petrol, and Myrtle sees him from the garage window, with Jordan in the passenger seat.

In the searing heat in a suite at the Plaza Hotel, music reminds Daisy of her romantic wedding day. Tom confronts Gatsby, revealing what he knows about Gatsby's lies and criminal activities. Shaken by these revelations, when each man tries to force her to declare that she loves only him, Daisy withdraws into herself and begs Tom to take her home. Tom contemptuously sends her back to East Egg with Gatsby, attempting to prove that his rival cannot hurt him.

When Nick, Jordan and Tom drive through the valley of ashes, they discover that Gatsby's car struck and killed Myrtle when she recognised the car Tom had been driving and ran towards it. They rush back to East Egg, where Nick learns from Gatsby that Daisy was driving the car, but that Gatsby intends to take the blame. The next day, Tom tells Myrtle's husband, George Wilson, that Gatsby was the driver of the car. By the time Nick reaches Gatsby's mansion after work, Gatsby is dead. He seems to have been shot as he lay on an air bed on the swimming pool. The discovery of George Wilson's body leads to the conclusion that he shot Gatsby and then himself.

The inquest comes to the obvious conclusion, but Nick suggests that this was to avoid uncovering the truth. Nick arranges Gatsby's funeral, ends his relationship with Jordan and moves back to the Midwest. Nick visits Gatsby's house one last time and experiences a moment of vision. Ever since the first settlers arrived, Americans have always had dreams which are doomed to be unachievable, and so Gatsby comes to stand for all American dreamers.

Commentary Nick comments that Tom had 'tanked up' at luncheon and was forcing Nick to accompany him. The 'supercilious assumption' was that Nick had nothing else to do. The slang term 'tanked up' implies that Tom had consumed a large quantity of alcohol and also compares him with a car; both Tom and a car have a large capacity and are very powerful. Using slang suggests contempt from the sober Nick, and his subsequent **Latinate polysyllabic** phrase 'supercilious assumption' both mocks Tom's heavy-handedness and conveys Nick's resentment.

The valley of ashes was Fitzgerald's name for the area around Flushing Creek acquired by the Brooklyn Ash Removal Company. The salt marshes were turned into a landfill site for garbage from the city and ashes from coal-burning furnaces. On one level it represents the grey, dismal environment of the Wilsons and their class, ignored and abandoned by the wealthy who pollute it. The valley is close to the lines of communication between the homes of the rich and the city, but the trains pass straight through, although forced to stop when barges are moving on the creek. Ironically, however, this 'dumping ground' is the inevitable end of the material possessions of the wealthy.

Fitzgerald calls the valley of ashes 'the waste land', which is the title of a poem by T.S. Eliot, published in 1922, three years before *The Great Gatsby*.

Both writers present readers with images of a barren landscape, where nothing grows. The valley of ashes seems to be watched over, but the eyes are not the eyes of God, just an abandoned advertisement, a symbol of materialism. Similarly, the Son of Man is neglected in Eliot's 'The Waste Land', where there is only 'a heap of broken images', suggesting discarded idols. Both worlds are spiritually dead and there is only 'fear in a handful of dust'. Fitzgerald sometimes refers to the ash as dust, and it echoes God's words to Adam and Eve: 'Dust thou art and to dust thou shalt return.' However, neither writer seems to interpret this as a fear of death; it is rather a fear of a meaningless life.

NB see also Commentary to Chapter VII on pages 17–19.

Myrtle's vitality becomes a 'violently affected' hauteur as she attempts to behave like a society hostess. She enters the apartment block 'haughtily', has furnished it with French tapestried furniture, complains about the servants and acts bored and blasé. However, there are individual details that are touching in their naïvety. She childishly refuses to travel in an ordinary taxi. She chooses a dog 'enthusiastically', strokes it 'with rapture', 'delicately' asks its gender, sends for straw and milk, kisses it 'with ecstasy', and then forgets about it, leaving it 'looking with blind eyes through the smoke and … groaning faintly'.

Nick mocks her movements because they lack natural grace and her voice that becomes mechanical with her efforts. Nick criticises her only for her social pretensions, not for her immoral behaviour; he never mocks her for being unfaithful to her husband. Nick's description of Myrtle as 'the despairing figure on the couch, bleeding fluently' sounds mocking; the adverb 'fluently' is usually associated with speech not blood, so he insensitively suggests she is creating a

Latinate: sophisticated words of Latin derivation.

polysyllabic: having more than two syllables.

Context

T.S. Eliot (1888–1965) was born in the United States but moved to England in 1914. His most significant work 'The Waste Land' (1922) expressed the disillusionment of the post-war generation with the hedonism of a materialistic society.

Build critical skills

Nick thought Fifth Avenue looked 'warm and soft, almost pastoral' and he 'wouldn't have been surprised to see a great flock of white sheep' (p. 30). What is Fitzgerald suggesting about how Nick perceives his surroundings?

ironic counterpoint: a contrasting image which serves to draw attention to the main image. Myrtle's red dress reflects her vitality as well as her infidelity and contrasts with Daisy in white. Both women are lying down, but Myrtle's nose has been broken by Tom and she is bleeding 'fluently', whereas Daisy is too hot and indolent to stand up and she does not speak fluently.

disproportionate fuss. This image provides an **ironic counterpoint** to Jordan and Daisy in Chapter I, reclining languorously on their couches in their white dresses. Whereas Tom bruises Daisy's finger without meaning to, he deliberately hits Myrtle so hard that he breaks her nose. She goes home with 'her face bruised and her nose swollen', but the absence of a dressing suggests that Tom did not take her to hospital (p. 149).

Nick's unflattering description of Catherine reveals his snobbery, especially in the pompous way he describes her plucked eyebrows growing back: 'the efforts of nature toward the restoration of the old alignment gave a blurred air to her face.' Catherine provides another reference to the mystery surrounding Gatsby, saying she is scared of him and reporting the rumour that he is related to Kaiser Wilhelm.

CRITICAL VIEW

In 1979, Keath Fraser argued for an acknowledgement of 'the full play of sexuality' in this erotically anarchic novel of 'potency and impotency, of jealous sex and Platonic love'. To support his thesis, he analysed Nick's fascination with Tom's masculine body as well as the homoerotic undertones in the scene between Nick and Chester McKee.

Chapter III

At one of Gatsby's parties, Nick hears rumours about his host before eventually meeting him and realising they served in the same division during the Great War. Gatsby has a private conversation with Jordan, who tells Nick that Gatsby has told her something amazing. Nick glosses over the next few weeks, describing his routine, admitting that he was growing to like New York and was gradually growing closer to Jordan.

Commentary Fitzgerald's impressionistic description of the party has a blend of long shots and close-up scenes. Observed first from Nick's house, we see both the stars and the coloured lights that 'make a Christmas tree of Gatsby's enormous garden'. 'The lights grow brighter as the earth lurches away from the sun', and the constantly changing artificial lights create 'a sea-change' of faces and voices and colour, as they illuminate the ever-moving crowds and blend them together, creating from a distance the effect of an ever-changing sea. Nick uses the term 'spectroscopic gaiety' to create the image of a prism, separating light into a whole spectrum of colours.

synaesthesia: the fusion of different sense impressions to enhance an experience.

Bright primary colours predominate and yellow seems the most dominant; even the cocktail music is yellow, an example of **synaesthesia** that suggests bright, cheerful, superficial music. The colours are 'gaudy', and Nick stands out because he is dressed in white, possibly symbolising his naïvety or his belief in his moral superiority.

Behind the conversations Nick reports, there is background music and the 'echolalia' provided by the party-goers. This term refers to a tendency to repeat words spoken by another, and so Fitzgerald conjures up a soundtrack of meaningless chatter against which one man is talking with 'curious intensity'.

West Egg is characterised by light, colour and energy, whereas the people who live in East Egg are conscious of their 'staid nobility' and are on their guard against any temptation to enjoy themselves. However, even they let their guard down and break under the influence of the champagne. The East Egg wife had seemed to be like a diamond – cool and hard by virtue of her wealth – but this was merely a pose, and she showed as much anger at her husband's behaviour as the West Egg wives.

The scene of the drunken car accident is **juxtaposed** with Nick's observation of 'a wafer of moon … shining over Gatsby's house'. Gatsby's dream remains intact and pure, symbolised by the moon rising above the garish lights of his drunken parties that 'blind' people literally and morally.

juxtapose: to place side by side.

A short linking passage reminds the readers that Nick is self-consciously crafting his narrative, and tells of another girl with whom he had an affair only to drop her when 'her brother began throwing mean looks'. He dreams of having secret romances with unknown women. For Nick, New York has a 'racy, adventurous feel … at night'; however, he feels 'a haunting loneliness sometimes' and, like the 'poor young clerks', he is an observer, 'wasting the most poignant moments of night and life'.

Chapter IV

Nick writes a list of the people he saw at Gatsby's parties. He is driven to Manhattan by Gatsby, who makes outrageous and well-rehearsed claims about his past. Nick is sceptical until Gatsby produces a photograph of himself at Oxford with an earl. Over lunch, Nick meets Meyer Wolfshiem, the gambler supposedly responsible for fixing the 1919 World Baseball Series. From Wolfshiem, Nick learns something of what happened to Gatsby when he returned from the war. Nick sees Tom and goes to introduce the two men, but Gatsby mysteriously disappears. The scene cuts abruptly to the Plaza Hotel, where Jordan takes over narration. She tells Nick that Daisy went out with Gatsby in Louisville, Kentucky, before he went to the war. In June 1919, she married Tom, who was unfaithful to her within three months of the wedding. Gatsby apparently bought his house to be across the bay from Daisy, and he would like to meet Daisy at Nick's bungalow.

Commentary

NB see **Writer's methods: Structure** from page 48 for a discussion about Nick's list.

NB see **Extended commentaries** on pages 97–8 for an analysis of Gatsby's car.

As Gatsby drove recklessly through Astoria in his 'gorgeous' automobile, a 'frantic policeman' tried unsuccessfully to stop him. When Gatsby was recognised, the policeman apologised. This light, even humorous, reference serves to make Fitzgerald's readers aware of corruption at the top of the New York police force.

NB see **Characters: Jay Gatsby** on pages 35–7 and **Writer's methods: Viewpoint** on pages 46–7 for some discussion about the conversation on the journey.

From a distance, the city looks like a fairytale landscape; however, even as he marvels at it, Nick is aware that it was 'built with a wish out of non-olfactory money', that those who paid for the buildings had gained their fortunes immorally. As they drive across Queensboro Bridge, the sunlight through the girders flickering on the cars contributes to its romantic appearance.

> **Build critical skills**
>
> Analyse how Gatsby cleverly prepares Nick for the 'big request' he has asked Jordan to put to him.

▲ Queensboro bridge, New York's 'first wild promise of all the mystery and the beauty in the world'

Fitzgerald juxtaposes the bright sunshine of 'roaring noon', and the dim lighting of a cellar in 'half-darkness'. In spite of Prohibition, alcohol is easy to obtain, and business is conducted in illegal drinking dens where people 'coolly' discuss immoral activities. These dens are not only frequented by the underworld; the apparently respectable Tom is also there. Setting the scene in bright sunshine adjacent to the poorly-lit cellar creates a strong visual image of the two sides of Gatsby: the flamboyant exterior which masks mysterious criminal activities.

Wolfshiem is a professional gambler; a dangerous man who uses a hitman to silence the opposition. This thug is appropriately named Katspaugh, a **homophone** for cat's paw.

> **Homophone**: a play on words involving two words or phrases that sound the same but are spelt differently.

Nick's mocking anti-Semitism means that Wolfshiem seems quite a comic character with his 'tragic nose' and his 'business gonnegtion'; the last word deliberately misspelt to emphasise Wolfshiem's pronunciation of the word 'connection'. However, Wolfshiem's name brands him a ruthless predator, and his cufflinks suggest sinister associations. Fitzgerald sets him firmly in the contemporary criminal fraternity by claiming that he was responsible for fixing the World's Baseball Series in 1919 and by linking him with 'Rosy' Rosenthal, a real gambler who was gunned down by the police.

Context

Herman Rosenthal complained to the press in 1912 that his illegal casinos had been badly damaged by the greed of the corrupt New York police who extorted money in exchange for immunity from police interference. Two days later he was gunned down outside the Hotel Metropole. Five police officers went to the electric chair for arranging the murder.

Jordan sits up 'very straight on a straight chair' as she tells Daisy's story, suggesting that her story will be 'straight' and she is to be trusted. When they drive through Central Park they hear a popular song about a sheik with his 'captured bride' and his plans to 'conquer love by fear'. In a telling critique on this age of mass entertainment, Fitzgerald has this brutal song being inappropriately sung by children.

Build critical skills

Research the Francis Cugat cover of *The Great Gatsby* online. What does this cover by Francis Cugat suggest about Nick that he felt he had to explain that: **'I had no girl whose disembodied face floated along the dark cornices and blinding signs'** (p. 78).

Context

In August 1924, Fitzgerald wrote to his publisher: 'For Christ sake, don't give anyone that jacket you're saving for me. I've written it into the book.' Why do you think Fitzgerald felt that this image was so important?

Chapter V

Gatsby is waiting for Nick on his return. He offers Nick some business on the side, which Nick interprets as an offer 'for services rendered'. He refuses. Structurally, Nick's tea party is at the centre of the novel. It rains, but the sun comes out briefly. Gatsby is embarrassed, then filled with 'unreasoning joy', then 'consumed with wonder at her presence'. He shows Daisy and Nick his house and grounds. Nick wonders whether Daisy can live up to Gatsby's dream of her. He leaves them holding hands.

Commentary Nick returns to West Egg at two o'clock in the morning. Gatsby is waiting to know whether Nick will invite Daisy to visit. He tries to appear nonchalant. As if to reinforce the message that his dream is not pure, the house appears to be winking conspiratorially as he tries to persuade Nick to act as go-between in his seduction of a married woman.

Context

In the infamous Black Sox Scandal of 1919, some members of the Chicago White Sox baseball team accepted bribes to lose games so that the Cincinnati Reds would win and make bookmakers a fortune. In 1988, a film of this scandal was released: *Eight Men Out*.

> Top ten quotation

Taking it further ▶

Research and read the lyrics of 'The Sheik of Araby' online. What do they suggest about Gatsby's intentions?

CRITICAL VIEW

'The actual meeting of Gatsby and Daisy is the central episode of the novel. Everything leads up to it, and what follows is a working out of the implications which are in the meeting itself'. (A.E. Dyson, '*The Great Gatsby*: Thirty-Six Years After', 1961)

On the day of the tea party, it is raining and the windows are 'bleared', symbolising Nick's inability to see clearly the immorality of his actions. The rain reflects Gatsby's apprehensive mood as he sits 'miserably' waiting for Daisy's arrival. Later, however, the sun comes out, reflecting Gatsby's change of mood. The childish synaesthesia in 'twinkle-bells of sunshine' enhances Nick's description of Gatsby as 'an ecstatic patron of recurrent light' and gives a veneer of childlike innocence to the scene.

Daisy lingers to enjoy the scents of the flowers as they approach Gatsby's house and waxes lyrical at the sunset peeping through the rain. When she sees Gatsby's shirts, her reaction is to cry 'stormily', suggesting there are deep emotions Nick cannot begin to understand. It is significant that Nick speculates what Gatsby is thinking about and tries to interpret his every expression, but reports Daisy's words and actions superficially.

Through Daisy's presence, Nick is able to appreciate the romantic atmosphere of the house and garden. When there is no party, the garden is filled with natural odours that are 'sparkling', 'frothy' or 'pale gold'. Fitzgerald's use of synaesthesia here fuses the senses of sight and smell to add depth to Nick's appreciation of the flowers. The bedrooms are vivid with new flowers and swathed in rose and lavender silk, subtle, feminine colours that suggest that inside the house is also fragrant and romantic.

Daisy is glowing; the sunlight gleams on her brass buttons and blinds Gatsby as it is reflected off the brush she is using. Nick describes Gatsby's shirts in subtle pastel shades using colours associated with natural things such as coral, apple-green, lavender and faint orange. Gatsby is wearing a white flannel suit, silver shirt and gold-coloured tie, which reinforces the idea of his feelings for her being pure, especially as his clothes echo the colours of a daisy that she wears so often. On this occasion, Daisy is wearing a lavender hat and her naturally blond hair 'lay like a dash of blue paint'. Clearly she has dyed her hair, which contradicts the fresh, natural image of her.

Taking it further ▶

Read the lyrics of 'The Love Nest' online.

What does Fitzgerald hope to achieve by the reference to this song, which would have been very well known when the novel was first published?

It starts to rain again, suggesting, perhaps, that the relationship is doomed. However, 'in the west … there was a pink and golden billow of foamy cloud', a romantic interval in an otherwise threatening sky. Gatsby attempts to banish the gloom by turning on the lights, but, in the music room, he turns on 'a solitary lamp'. The flame on the match with which he nervously lights Daisy's cigarette trembles, and he and Daisy sit in the shadows where there is 'no light save what the gleaming floor bounced in from the hall'. This image echoes Keats' 'Ode to a Nightingale', but the light is artificial, and thunder can be heard ominously rumbling outside, as if Nature herself disapproves (see **Themes: Urban Romanticism** on page 28 for a full analysis of this image).

The lighting reinforces the negative note of the songs Klipspringer plays, and reminds us that Gatsby 'had no real right to touch her hand'. Klipspringer first plays 'The Love Nest' on the piano.

Nick leaves while Klipspringer is playing 'Ain't We Got fun', a jolly, popular tune.

Fitzgerald quotes from the lyrics to reinforce his message that the careless, hedonistic lifestyle of the rich can only be temporary, 'in between time'. The explicit class division offers an ironic commentary on the class difference between Daisy and Gatsby as they are, presumably, about to make love. The lyrics highlight the carelessness of the rich as they joke about the plight of the poor, just as the novel highlights their carelessness to the hopelessness of those in the valley of ashes.

Chapter VI

Nick deviates from his plan to tell events in the order in which he learns them and narrates some of what Gatsby supposedly tells him the night after Myrtle is killed. We learn that Gatsby was the son of a small farmer. He was dissatisfied with his life, left home and drifted until, at 17, he met Dan Cody.

Nick describes an occasion when Tom and friends rode over to Gatsby's house. Gatsby is a welcoming and generous host, and Mrs Sloane issues an empty invitation which Gatsby gratefully accepts. When he goes to get his car, they rudely ride away. Tom and Daisy go to Gatsby's next party and Nick senses a 'pervading harshness that hadn't been there before'. After the party, Nick interprets in his own words what Gatsby told him of his affair with Daisy.

Commentary Another linking passage reinforces our awareness of Gatsby as a criminal. A reporter is exploring rumours that Gatsby is linked to an underground pipeline bringing alcohol from Canada. Nick dismisses the rumours as 'inventions', refusing to see what must have been obvious.

Nick asserts, categorically, that 'The truth was that Jay Gatsby of West Egg, Long Island, sprang from his Platonic conception of himself.' The Greek philosopher, Plato, suggested that the material world we experience is a mere shadow of some higher realm of transcendent ideas or forms. Nick seems to be suggesting that James Gatz had already created his own identity as an ideal conception of himself and could produce this new identity, ready-made, in the time it took him to row to Cody's yacht.

NB for an analysis of Nick's description of James Gatz's dreams see **Top ten quotations** on page 101.

Nick's description of Cody helps to explain the contrast between East and West. Cody made his fortune in the West and 'brought back to the Eastern seaboard the savage violence of the frontier brothel and saloon'. Cody gave Gatsby a taste for wealth and a dubious moral stance on how to obtain it.

The 'sinister contrast' between East and West Egg could be that the residents of East Egg are unable to seize the day and live a life of 'euphemisms' in which the truth, like Tom's mistress, is known but not spoken about. A prime example is when Mrs Sloane enthusiastically invites Gatsby and Nick to supper; Nick is familiar with the code and knows she does not mean it, but Gatsby belongs to

Taking it further

Read the lyrics to 'Ain't We Got Fun' online.

Is there anything significant in the lyrics Fitzgerald does not quote but would have expected his readers to be familiar with?

Build critical skills

Fitzgerald writes that Cody had given Gatsby 'his singularly appropriate education'. What do you think he means by this?

Build critical skills

How much of the first four pages of this chapter do you think is Gatsby's description, and how much is Nick's imaginative reconstruction?

Taking it further ▶

Look at a map of North America and consider how likely it is that a pre-war luxury yacht would be able to sail round the continent. Can you suggest different interpretations of why Gatsby might claim this?

Build critical skills

At the first party, Nick mentions five crates of oranges and lemons. This time he notices only 'fruit rinds and discarded flowers'. What does this detail suggest about his changing attitudes?

West Egg and takes her invitation at face value. Nick is outraged at the cruel humiliation inflicted on his friend, putting an exclamation mark after his bitter comment: 'As though they cared!'

Nick uses more muted colours for the party than in his description in Chapter III. The producer has a 'sort of blue nose'; the 'ghostly' celebrity is 'a gorgeous, scarcely human orchid of a woman', and she sits under 'a white-plum tree'. The morning is 'soft black', and 'sometimes a shadow moved against a dressing-room blind above, gave way to another shadow, an indefinite procession of shadows'. Even the beach is black. The unpleasantness Nick feels could be because he identifies with Gatsby's humiliation and resents how he is being used by his guests.

Daisy embraces the spirit of the party; she keeps a check on Tom but relaxes when she sees the girl he is with is no real threat. Once again Nick is complicit in her affair with Gatsby, keeping watch while the lovers retire to his house. West Egg stands for vigour, energy, novelty and escapism, in opposition to the moribund East Egg. Daisy may not approve of the people of West Egg, but she says 'At least they are more interesting than the people we know.'

Nick's perception is that the lives of these newly rich are empty and that a force beyond their control, 'fate', is herding them like cattle 'from nothing to nothing'. However, they know this and enjoy their lives without worrying about the future. This seems to be the 'very simplicity' that he thinks Daisy failed to understand.

Taking it further ▶▶

After character names, the word 'time' is the second-most frequently used noun in *The Great Gatsby*. Read the lyrics to 'Three o'Clock in the Morning' online and consider why this is an appropriate song at this point in the novel.

▲ "Three o'Clock in the Morning" a neat, sad little waltz of that year'

Chapter VII

On the hottest day of the summer, Nick has lunch at the Buchanans'. Aimlessly, they drive to Manhattan, with Daisy and Gatsby in Tom's car and the others in Gatsby's. Tom stops at Wilson's garage for petrol, and Myrtle sees him with Jordan. In the unbearable heat in the Plaza Hotel, tensions rise, and Tom challenges Gatsby to explain himself. Gatsby tries to make Daisy say that she never loved Tom, but she will not do this. Nevertheless, she does say she is leaving Tom, and this provokes him to give details of Gatsby's criminal activities. Gatsby ends up 'defending his name against accusations that had not been made'. This frightens Daisy, and she draws into herself, now powerless to do anything. Tom, realising he has won, scornfully tells Daisy to go home with Gatsby.

Nick's narrative uses the evidence of Michaelis (Wilson's friend and neighbour who cares for Wilson in the aftermath of Myrtle's death) at the inquest to fill in the details of what happened before Myrtle recognised the car Tom had been driving and rushed out to her death. Michaelis gives a graphic description of the body. Nick then resumes his supposed eye-witness account of their arrival at the garage where Myrtle is already dead.

Back at the Buchanans', Nick resists invitations to go in. He sees Gatsby watching the house. From what Gatsby says, he guesses Daisy was driving. He peeps into the house and sees Daisy and Tom together, with Tom's hand resting casually on Daisy's as he talks.

Commentary Nick's reference to Gatsby as Trimalchio once again links *The Great Gatsby* with Eliot's 'The Waste Land', which has a quotation from the *Satyricon* as the epigraph. In Eliot's chosen extract, the nouveau-riche narrator describes how he saw the Cumaean Sybil in a glass bottle being taunted by boys. When Apollo had granted her a wish, she had asked for as many years of life as she held grains of sand in her hand. However, she forgot to ask for continuous youth. It is significant that both writers foresee the dangers in a barren life that is concerned only with material things and has no spiritual dimension at all.

Gatsby dismisses his servants and replaces them with Wolfshiem's thugs. While Daisy and Gatsby conduct their love affair there will be constant reminders of the criminal activities through which Gatsby gained entry to Daisy's world. If the kitchen looked like 'a pigsty' and the general opinion in the village is that they are not servants, it is very unlikely that they used to run a small hotel, as Gatsby claims.

Nick jumps to the conclusion that Myrtle thinks Jordan is Tom's wife when she looks at the car 'with jealous terror'; however, she has probably seen pictures of Daisy in society magazines, and she would be unlikely to be jealous seeing Tom with his wife. She must fear that Tom has a new mistress.

Context

Fitzgerald considered calling the novel *Trimalchio at West Egg*. Trimalchio is the narrator of the *Satyricon* by Petronius, a satire on Roman life in the first century AD. A freed slave who became wealthy, he was renowned for excessively lavish parties.

Build critical skills

How far do you think Fitzgerald has been limited by the personality of his narrator? In what ways would *The Great Gatsby* be a different novel if Jordan had been the narrator?

Fitzgerald makes his readers feel the heat. He takes us inside the Buchanans' house where 'the room, shadowed well with awnings, was dark and cool', the dining-room too was 'darkened against the heat'. However, Fitzgerald needs the party to drive past the garage and the heat to shorten tempers, so they travel to Manhattan, where there is no cool refuge. As the men wait for the women, Nick notices 'a silver curve of the moon' in the western sky, but the brightness of the sun, which makes pebbles blaze, will symbolically drain this romantic image of any light at all.

NB for an analysis of the way Fitzgerald makes his readers feel the heat, see **Writer's methods: The heat and the sweat** on page 62.

When the row that has been brewing eventually erupts, Gatsby appears 'content', but Daisy looks 'desperately from one to the other', although earlier she seemed to be trying to provoke it. Perhaps Mendelssohn's 'Wedding March' reminded her why she married Tom and rekindled the love she had for him then. Put on the spot, she realises that she and Tom share happy memories she cannot deny. When Tom starts giving details of how Gatsby made his money, Daisy is 'terrified'. Confronted with his illegal and amoral activities, she draws back into herself. When Gatsby reveals even more crimes by defending himself 'against accusations that had not been made', she turns to Tom to protect her. It seems she had wanted love and romance not a life of sordid crime. She is 'alarmed' when Tom insists she drive back with Gatsby. She is vulnerable, but Tom is showing off his victory by insisting she spend time alone with his rival.

When they have left, Nick inopportunely announces that it is his thirtieth birthday, 'the promise of a decade of loneliness, a thinning list of single men to know, a thinning briefcase of enthusiasm, thinning hair'. Through this repetitive list, Fitzgerald makes his readers aware how empty his narrator's life is, and that he has no strong feelings for Jordan.

Confused and upset, Daisy asks to drive, possibly to steady her nerves, as Gatsby claims. Gatsby's car is powerful, and Daisy finds it difficult to control. When Myrtle runs out, Daisy hesitates. She swerves away into the path of an oncoming car and then back to avoid a collision. When she hits Myrtle, she steps on the accelerator and cannot stop, although whether this is through fear or because she cannot control the vehicle is unclear. When Gatsby pulls on the emergency brake, she collapses, clearly emotionally overwrought.

foreshadow: to arrange events and information so that later events are prepared for.

When Tom, Nick and Jordan reach the scene, it is evening. The garage is 'lit only by a yellow light in a swinging metal basket overhead'. As the light swings, Nick sees Wilson swaying in the doorway of his office. Wilson seems mesmerised by the light, looking from it to Myrtle and then back, calling out incessantly: 'Oh, my Ga-od!' This **foreshadows** the fragment that Michaelis describes, when the eyes of Dr Eckleburg begin to emerge, pale and enormous, in the dawn light, and Wilson repeats 'God sees everything'. The lighting of both scenes suggests that Wilson feels a need for something to give meaning to life and death, but there is no God, only an artificial light and an advertisement.

NB for an analysis of the description of Myrtle's body, see **Building skills 2: Analysing texts in detail** on page 92.

At the Buchanans' mansion, two windows are 'bloomed with light'. The use of the verb 'bloom' suggests a natural flower-like quality, but it is electric light, in contrast with the moonlight outside. The lighting associates Daisy with the *illusion* of romance, whereas Gatsby is bathed in moonlight as he watches over the woman he loves in a sacred 'vigil'.

Jordan swallows her pride and twice invites Nick in. He has led her to believe that his intentions are serious, even ingratiating himself with her aunt; now, when she needs him, he fails her. Nick swears at the memory: 'I'd be damned if I'd go in', and he turns instead to Gatsby.

Peering through the pantry window and below the closed blind, Nick sees Daisy and Tom and assumes that for Daisy the romance is over, and she has returned to her safe, rich world, leaving Gatsby, symbolically lit by moonlight, 'watching over nothing'. Fitzgerald's use of the moon associates Gatsby with romantic heroes and pure love, while the artificial light that draws Tom and Daisy together suggests that Daisy has betrayed her lover.

Chapter VIII

Before dawn, Nick goes across to Gatsby's house. Nick paraphrases what Gatsby tells him about his wartime love affair with Daisy, and what he did when he returned from the war. Nick feels close to Gatsby as he leaves. At the office, Jordan phones asking to see him. He declines. He tries unsuccessfully to phone Gatsby four times. Once again Nick deviates from his plan and tells us what he learned later, at the inquest and from the newspapers. He gives the details of Wilson's movements the day after Myrtle was killed, however, he withholds the information that Wilson called at the Buchanans' house. Nick then reconstructs Gatsby's last movements and tries to imagine his feelings as he lay on the air bed. Although Nick was one of the people who found Gatsby, he gives no description of the body, and mentions only that the gardener found Wilson's body, so we are given no graphic descriptions of these violent deaths.

Commentary No longer are Nick's dreams of romantic women smiling invitingly at him. Now he tosses 'half-sick between grotesque reality and savage, frightening dreams'. What is keeping him awake is fear that there will be repercussions for Gatsby after Myrtle's death. When he hears Gatsby return, he jumps out of bed to warn him, but Gatsby is clutching 'at some last hope'. With only the glow of the cigarettes illuminating their faces, Gatsby tells Nick the story of how he came to be following a '**grail**', like the heroes of medieval romances. At dawn, Fitzgerald is very specific about the quality of the 'grey-turning, gold-turning' light that fills the house, a gloomy light, but still with a hint of gold to suggest the possibility of romance.

Context

In a letter to his publisher in 1924, Fitzgerald wrote: 'Chapter VII will never quite be up to the mark - I've worried about it too long, and I can't quite place Daisy's reaction.'

Taking it further ▶

'Beale Street Blues' (p. 143) is a lament that Prohibition threatened the life of this colourful place. In Beale Street, Tennessee, music expressed the dreams and the heartache of people who had recently been slaves; this was where the Blues were born. Read the lyrics online and consider why Fitzgerald has included this song.

Top ten quotation

NB for a comparative analysis of Gatsby's account of falling in love with Daisy and Nick's interpretation, see **Building skills 2**: **Analysing texts in detail** on pages 93–4.

In a description of Gatsby's smile, Nick juxtaposes the rapturous word 'ecstatic', derived from the ancient Greek word for standing outside oneself, with the rough slang term 'cahoots'. This phrase neatly sums up Nick's perception of Gatsby, the 'elegant young rough-neck' with the sublime dream. The fact that Nick does not think they have been in league with each other all along reveals that he neither realises how he has been used nor admits his part in the affair.

When Jordan telephones Nick the following day, her voice, usually fresh and cool, 'seemed harsh and dry' over the phone, suggesting that she is under emotional strain.

NB see **Characters** for further analysis of this telephone call on page 42.

Fitzgerald employs **dramatic irony** when Nick replies, 'I want to see you, too' because we know he is lying. She takes his words at face value and suggests abandoning her plans to go to Southampton to meet him, revealing how desperately she needs to see him. Nick is annoyed that Jordan has left Daisy's house, but he does not ask why. Jordan went because Daisy and Tom left the house after Tom told Wilson where to find the driver of the yellow car. Significantly, Fitzgerald withholds this information until the end of the novel.

After Gatsby's death, Nick assumes he was waiting for a phone call from Daisy. However, Fitzgerald creates mystery because, when Nick tried to phone Gatsby that morning, 'the wire was being kept open for a long distance from Detroit'. Perhaps Daisy did try to phone. Perhaps Gatsby was still waiting for the call from Detroit.

NB for an analysis of Nick's description of what he saw at Gatsby's house see **Extended commentaries** on pages 99–100.

> **dramatic irony**: when the reader knows something the character speaking does not and this creates tension or humour.

Context

Southampton, Long Island, is the home of the National Golf Links of America.

Chapter IX

Nick spent a year writing his account of events. In the final chapter, he tells what he remembers. He refers to the inquest and mentions learning that Daisy and Tom had gone away. He tried to persuade Wolfshiem to go to the funeral, and he describes a strange phone call that implicated Gatsby in a bond fraud. On the third day, Gatsby's father arrives and details of Gatsby's early life are revealed. Nick decides to go home. He says goodbye to Jordan and challenges Tom about sending Wilson to Gatsby but then shakes his hand. He visits Gatsby's deserted house. Lying on the shore in the moonlight, he has a vision of Long Island as it would have looked to the Dutch sailors who first discovered it, promising a new life in a new world, just as the green light at the end of Daisy's dock had promised Gatsby that he could achieve his dream. Nick realises that, although these dreams are forever out of reach because they are based on a vision of lost innocence, it will not stop us striving for them.

Commentary Nick is now remembering events which happened two years before. He has supposedly taken more than a year to craft his narrative, and there is evidence of his fanciful imagination in the way he describes Gatsby's corpse seeming to talk to him.

NB see **Building skills 2: Analysing texts in detail** from page 93. for two student answers about Gatsby's father.

Gatsby's father is clearly proud of his son. It may have been he who made James Gatz ambitious, as he is convinced that, had his son lived, he would have 'helped build up the country'. His dream, like that of the Founding Fathers, was to make America great.

NB see **Historical context: The American Dream** on page 66.

As Nick thinks of returning to the Midwest, where old traditions and family values have offered security in the past, he recalls other times when he returned home from school and college.

NB for an analysis of his recollections, see **Themes: East and West** on pages 25–6.

Nick remembers that, when he returned from the war, the East had excited him. At that time, he found the Midwest stifling with the 'interminable inquisitions' and the East had offered a fresh start, but 'after Gatsby's death the East was haunted' for him, like the nightmare scenes El Greco painted, so he decided to 'come back home'. Using **pathetic fallacy**, Fitzgerald projects Nick's mood onto the 'sullen' sky, and the moon is 'lustreless', with no suggestion of romance.

pathetic fallacy: attributing human emotions or attributes to elements of nature.

Taking it further ▷

Study this painting and others by El Greco and consider what insights this reference gives into Nick's nightmares.

CRITICAL VIEW

'Insofar as it is the narrator's story, it is a successful transcendence of a particularly bitter and harrowing set of experiences, localised in the sinister, distorted El Greco-like Long Island atmosphere of the later twenties, into a world of restored sanity and calm, symbolised by the bracing winter nights of the Middle Western prairies.' (William Troy, 'Fitzgerald – the Authority of Failure', *Accent* magazine, 1945)

The final fragment Fitzgerald offers is of Nick's last night in West Egg, looking out over the Sound. As the moon rises higher and shines more brightly, the details of the scene fade away until he has a vision of what the island must have looked like when the Dutch sailors first arrived, and he imagines how they felt when they saw '**a fresh green breast of the new world**'. Here Fitzgerald fuses the dreams of the first explorers with Gatsby's dream 'when he first picked out the green light at the end of Daisy's dock', and then the light becomes a symbol of the American Dream of '**the orgastic future that year by year recedes before us**'.

> Top ten quotation

> Top ten quotation

TASK

Put the following events in the correct order:

1 Tom and Daisy settle in Chicago.

2 Tom and Daisy stay at a hotel in Santa Barbara.

3 Tom and Daisy go to France for a year.

4 Tom and Daisy go to the South Seas.

5 Tom and Daisy settle in East Egg.

6 Pammy is born.

Target your thinking

- What is your response to the ways in which women are presented in the novel? (**AO1**)
- In what ways has Fitzgerald demonstrated the flaw at the heart of the American Dream? (**AO3**)
- How does Fitzgerald suggest that appearances are not always what they seem to be and different interpretations are possible? (**AO5**)

As this diagram shows, the themes are all interlinked, and crucial to them all is the fact that the novel is set at a particular time in history, shortly after the Great War.

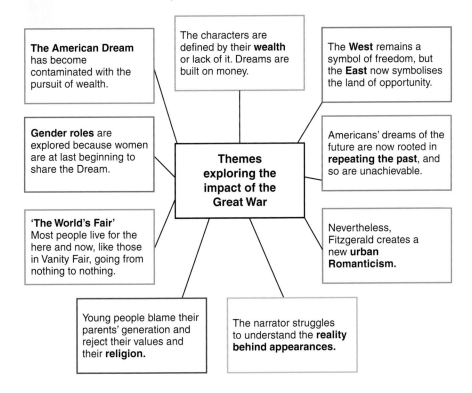

The American Dream has become contaminated with the pursuit of wealth.

The characters are defined by their **wealth** or lack of it. Dreams are built on money.

The **West** remains a symbol of freedom, but the **East** now symbolises the land of opportunity.

Gender roles are explored because women are at last beginning to share the Dream.

Themes exploring the impact of the Great War

Americans' dreams of the future are now rooted in **repeating the past**, and so are unachievable.

'The World's Fair' Most people live for the here and now, like those in Vanity Fair, going from nothing to nothing.

Nevertheless, Fitzgerald creates a new **urban Romanticism.**

Young people blame their parents' generation and reject their values and their **religion.**

The narrator struggles to understand the **reality behind appearances.**

The American Dream

The American Dream is rooted in the American Declaration of Independence (1776) and its insistence on 'all men' (significantly not women) having the right to the 'Pursuit of Happiness'. However, if happiness is defined as a 'right' and regarded as an entitlement like 'life' and 'liberty', then the Declaration can too readily be interpreted as justifying the actions of those who pursue wealth at any cost.

The Founding Fathers, who signed the Declaration, saw America as a blank slate upon which they could create their vision of a perfect state, free from the inequalities of life in the Old World. They wanted to create a land of opportunity where success depended not on birth or privilege but on hard work and courage. However, this worthy ideal soon proved unworkable and led to the bitterness of failure and disappointment for many of those who embraced its ethos.

Fitzgerald uses Dan Cody, the pioneer, to illustrate the flaws in the American Dream. Cody's wealth was supposedly 'a product of the Nevada silver fields, of the Yukon, of every rush for metal since seventy-five'. Prospecting did create millionaires, but the mania to get rich brought out the worst in human nature. Cody would seem to be the antithesis of the American Dream yet in fact represents the hard reality. Idealism and hope are essential ingredients of American history, but they have always gone hand in hand with exploitation and a desire for profit. The pioneers pushed westward, partly out of the excitement of exploration and discovery, but also in the hope of wealth; the unknown interior, with huge tracts of fertile land awaiting claimants, represented their dream of a new life.

In the twentieth century, men like Gatsby got rich quickly, but Fitzgerald writes of the '**foul dust**' that '**floated in the wake of his dreams**', illustrating that Gatsby's methods sit uneasily with the romance of his dream.

Context

Daniel Boone was famous for winning Kentucky from the Native Americans. Buffalo Bill Cody was a soldier and showman, who earned his nickname by killing 4,280 buffalo in 18 months.

Top ten quotation

Wealth

The Great Gatsby is full of money, and the reader is permitted to glimpse the extravagant lifestyle of the fabulously wealthy. However, Fitzgerald has exposed the reality behind the façade. In this society everyone is defined by their wealth and, importantly, when it was acquired. There is a sharp division between the inhabitants of East Egg with their 'old money' and those of West Egg with 'new money', but both are going from 'nothing to nothing'. Both communities live in close proximity to the desperate poverty of those in the valley of ashes, and have to travel through the valley every time they go into New York.

Nick judges that New York was built with 'non-olfactory money', acquired by immoral means. However, Nick's family's money comes from a business built up when his great uncle paid for a substitute to fight for him in the American Civil War; it was self-interest and the exploitation of a poorer man that set up Nick's 'prominent, well-to-do' family. Tom is from Chicago, so his family probably made their money in the infamous meat trade. Gatsby's dream is built on the money he had to acquire to reach Daisy, but his ruthless methods of acquiring it frighten her away.

Manhattan is where the gambler and criminal businessman, Meyer Wolfshiem, has his office. Manhattan is also the financial centre where Nick is learning about the bond business. Although the word 'bond' suggests honour and dependability, bonds are only a substitute for real money, and in the 1920s they were sold 'on the margin', to people who could not afford to pay for them but intended to pay their creditor out of the profits when the shares were sold.

East and West

Early settlers from Europe travelled West to the New World. They settled on the Eastern Seaboard but, for Americans, the West has always been a powerful symbol of opportunity and freedom. If you are travelling West, you are following the path of the sun which sets in the West, and so the West is the end of the trail and the pioneers' journeys, their hopes and dreams.

Life for the pioneers who pushed forward the frontier of civilisation in the Wild West was hard, and the law was difficult to enforce, so they developed a distinctive American spirit, very different from those who remained in the East, where the influence of the Old World was stronger. Dan Cody represents these pioneers, having made his fortune using unscrupulous methods. Fitzgerald notes that he gave Gatsby a 'singularly appropriate education', implying that Gatsby brought the values of the Wild West to his dealings in the East.

The pioneers were survivors, and Nick suggests that the harshness of their lives had destroyed their sense of the 'fundamental decencies'. When the continent was 'tamed', its mineral wealth exploited and the West Coast populated, there were no longer so many opportunities to make one's fortune, so the same ruthless men turned East. The West remained a symbol of freedom, but the financial and business world on the Eastern Seaboard came to symbolise the opportunity to make money quickly.

East and West Eggs

Fitzgerald employed the symbolism of East and West when he renamed Great Neck and Manhasset Neck as West and East Egg. Like the Wild West, West Egg was a place for opportunists, who had made their money in entertainment or racketeering. By contrast, East Egg was the fashionable part of Long Island where the wealthy descendants of people who had made their money in the previous century lived.

NB see also **Writer's methods: Symbolic settings** on pages 56–8 and **Commentary to Chapter III** on pages 10–11.

The Midwest

For Nick, the Midwest represents old-fashioned family values. Nick belongs to an extended family, the members of which all participate in the decision-making and share a family business. Until he went away to war, the Midwest had been the warm centre of Nick's world. However, when he returned from the war, the Midwest had 'seemed like the ragged end of the universe'.

After Gatsby's death, Nick decided to 'come back home', the verb 'come' rather than 'go' suggesting that he feels that the Midwest is where he belongs.

He recalls other times when he returned home from school and college. He remembers a sense of collective belonging which is revealed in his use of plural first person possessive determiners: 'our identity with this country', 'our snow'; and a personal attachment with 'my Middle West', 'I am part of that'. His memories are of friends, Christmas festivities and long train journeys; however, what he remembers is not the reality but a Christmas card scene which suggests the innocent world of childhood when even long train journeys were 'thrilling'. Fitzgerald suggests that Nick is also hoping to repeat the past.

Repeating the past

The Romantic poets were fascinated by time, and Keats especially explored different ways of trying to defeat time in his poetry. 'Ode on a Grecian Urn' celebrates the way in which sculptors can defeat time by freezing a moment so successfully that, in our imaginations, we can use all our senses to experience that moment and enhance it. In a similar way to the sculptor, Fitzgerald the novelist has captured the mood of post-war New York in the summer of 1922 and frozen it forever so that we can feel, hear and see the Jazz Age as we read his novels.

In *The Great Gatsby*, Fitzgerald takes up this theme of the Romantics and explores man's attempts to repeat the past. Gatsby has rewritten his past, having manipulated time once when he reinvented himself, and he dreams of doing it again. Fitzgerald, however, demonstrates through other characters that many post-war Americans share this dream.

Time

TASK

What evidence can you find that Nick is checking his watch at the party?

Nick never manages to give himself up totally to the Roaring Twenties. He cannot relax and give himself to the moment, as the other guests at Gatsby's party do; he is constantly watching the clock and aware of time passing. In Chapter III, he describes the party in an impressionistic way, mingling colours, sounds and lights. However, he underpins his impressions with the exactness of statistics and time, and this precision emphasises his place as an outsider, a watcher.

The orchestra plays Vladimir Tostoff's 'Jazz History of the World'. The invented name of the composer points to the ephemeral (short-lived) quality of the music – it was tossed off quickly – and perhaps the hedonistic lifestyles of New Yorkers in the 1920s, who want to toss history aside and live for the moment. Perhaps the paradoxical title – 'Jazz History of the World' – suggests people taking themselves too seriously or the difference between appearances and reality: while the history of the world sounds like an ambitious and important enterprise, this is undermined by it being expressed through jazz, which, in the early 1920s, was by many considered a lowly and even corrupting form of music. However, Nick keeps us aware that time is moving inexorably forward.

On page 56, Nick, the self-conscious narrator, realises that he has compressed time, and he takes the trouble to correct this impression and to give an account of his everyday activities. He is a man of routine, but he dreams romantic dreams and imagines that he too 'was hurrying towards gaiety' and sharing the intimate excitement of the theatre-goers. Fitzgerald has created a narrator whose Romantic soul is fascinated by Gatsby's pursuit of his dream, while his cautious, pedantic temperament keeps him in touch with reality.

Gatsby is determined to defeat time and resume the relationship he had with Daisy in the past. Symbolically, in his first meeting with her after nearly five years, Gatsby knocks a clock off the mantelpiece and catches it before it falls. For a moment, they all believe that the clock has smashed to pieces on the floor; the power of Gatsby's dream is made momentarily real by Daisy's presence, but the clock is returned to its place, and time continues to move forward.

At the moment when Gatsby's dream is fulfilled, and he is about to be alone with Daisy, Fitzgerald provides, as accompaniment to this romantic moment, a popular song which recognises the social injustice of a society in which 'the rich get rich and the poor get laid off'. The theme of the song is that the 'fun' is only temporary; only 'in the meantime, in between time' can Gatsby and Daisy relive the past.

When Gatsby was a teenager with romantic dreams, 'A universe of ineffable gaudiness spun itself out in his brain while the clock ticked on the washstand and the moon soaked with wet light his tangled clothes upon the floor' (pp. 95–6). Symbolically, Fitzgerald links Gatsby's dream world with moonlight; this may be a romantic image but the moon is actually an image of natural time, as it rises and sets regularly and changes in monthly cycles. To underline his point, Fitzgerald links young Gatsby's dream and the moonlight to the harsh ticking of a clock; the image is rooted in real-time and exposes Gatsby's dream as unreality.

Gatsby believes that it is possible to repeat the past; Nick gathered that Gatsby 'wanted to recover something, some idea of himself perhaps, that had gone into loving Daisy'. This reminds Nick of 'an elusive rhythm, a fragment of lost words, that I had heard somewhere a long time ago', but Nick cannot remember what it is: 'What I had almost remembered was incommunicable forever.' Both men seem to be trying to recapture a time of lost innocence. Fitzgerald suggests that repeating the past is a universal theme, and that we would all like to go back to a time when we had nothing to regret.

Nick believes that, when Gatsby first kissed Daisy, when he 'wed his unutterable visions to her perishable breath' (p. 107), he already knew that, unlike Keats' nightingale, the 'immortal Bird', Daisy is human and so unable to live up to his illusions. However, the kiss felt like the realisation of his dream. This is the turning point of Gatsby's life and starts his obsession to recreate that moment. However, we later learn that he 'made the most of his time. He took what he could get, ravenously and unscrupulously' (p.141). This indicates the ruthless opportunism which is at the heart of his pursuit of Daisy.

In the final sentence, '**So we beat on, boats against the current, borne back ceaselessly into the past**', Fitzgerald gives Nick the first person plural pronoun 'we' to involve us all in the realisation that the dreams towards which we stretch out our arms are inevitably out of reach because they are, in reality, irrecoverable visions of time past.

Taking it further ▶

Read Keats' 'Ode to a Nightingale'. It seems that the nightingale has defeated death because its song has always been present throughout history. Similarly, Nick describes Daisy's voice as a 'deathless song' (p. 93), giving Gatsby the illusion that he can defeat time and recreate the past.

CRITICAL VIEW

'Because the dream is unrealisable, the past becomes increasingly important to the book, for it is in memories that the dream can live.' (Roger Lewis, *Money, Love, and Aspiration in The Great Gatsby*, 1985)

Top ten quotation

Urban Romanticism

Fitzgerald chooses a narrator with a romantic imagination so that he can gloss over the means by which Gatsby became rich and concentrate on his dream instead. Nick, however, is not a Romantic in the nineteenth-century tradition; Fitzgerald reconstructed Romanticism to fit 1920s urban America. Nick uses romantic images to describe the city and urban locations. Fifth Avenue is 'warm and soft, almost pastoral' and a fitting backdrop for 'a great flock of white sheep'. The 'white chasms' in the artificial landscape of Manhattan are not gorges made by rivers but the spaces between white skyscrapers, and the 'metropolitan twilight' is 'enchanted'. In Daisy and Tom's house, the wind blew the curtains 'like pale flags, twisting them up toward the frosted wedding-cake of the ceiling, and then rippled over the wine-coloured rug, making a shadow on it as wind does on the sea'.

When Daisy imagines that she sees a nightingale, she knows it is not native to America and must have 'come over on the Cunard or White Star Line', a symbolic acknowledgement that Romanticism has had to adapt to American culture. Fitzgerald has combined twentieth-century American symbols of tragedy with the classical tragic image of Philomel, the nightingale, to give insight into the sadness beneath Daisy's 'tense gaiety'. The suggestion of her longing for romantic love adds **pathos** to the scene where the 'fifth guest's shrill metallic urgency' will not let her forget that Tom is unfaithful.

pathos: evocation of pity by a situation of suffering and helplessness.

Context

In classical mythology, Philomel, a tragic victim of male lust and brutality, was turned into a nightingale. Therefore, as well as being a romantic image, the bird carries associations with tragedy. The Cunard and White Star Lines also carry such associations because of the sinking of RMS *Lusitania* and RMS *Titanic*.

Fitzgerald uses a direct echo of 'Ode to a Nightingale' when Daisy and Nick visit Gatsby's house. While Keats listens to the bird's song, he is lying under trees; the moon is out, 'But here there is no light,/ Save what from heaven is with the breezes blown'. Nick observes that Daisy and Gatsby sit in a dark corner of the room, 'where there was no light save what the gleaming floor bounced in from the hall'. Instead of moonlight coming down from 'heaven', the light from an electric bulb in the hall is reflected upwards. Instead of the light being 'blown' naturally on the breezes, it is 'bounced' like a solid man-made object. As well as creating an Urban Romantic moment, the echo helps Fitzgerald to evoke the significance of the moment for the two lovers as they are alone for the first time in five years.

NB see also **Extended commentaries: Gatsby's death** on pages 99–100 and **Writer's methods: Patterns of imagery: The future** on page 58.

TASK

Find other examples of Fitzgerald's use of contemporary technology to evoke romantic images. Explore what you think he has achieved by doing this.

Reality behind appearances

Nick reports his sense impressions as events unfold, but he struggles to understand the reality behind them. He is our eyes; we see only what he notices and comments on. Nick is, by nature, an onlooker. In Chapter I, he wants to give the impression of being frank and open, 'to look squarely at every one, and yet to avoid all eyes', not wanting to get involved. When the telephone rang, he incomprehensibly says that his instinct was to telephone for the police. A possible explanation may be found in the following paragraph. Tom and Jordan stroll back into the library, 'as if to a vigil beside a perfectly tangible body'. To the over-imaginative Nick, the telephone call has killed something, and Tom and Jordan are going to keep watch and say prayers over it. Fitzgerald seems to be signalling to his readers that Nick has a tendency for **hyperbole**, and we should not take everything he says too literally.

In New York, Nick watches with a 'restless eye' and imagines rendezvous with romantic women (p. 57). When Tom and Daisy come to Gatsby's party, he feels an unpleasantness in the air and speculates that he is looking at the party, and at West Egg itself, through Daisy's eyes: 'It is invariably saddening to look through new eyes at things upon which you have expended your own powers of adjustment.' These are reminders to the reader that he is not an omniscient narrator, and that everything he writes is filtered through his own vision and insight, or lack of it.

After Gatsby's death, Nick realises that 'the East was haunted for me … distorted beyond my eyes' power of correction', reminding the reader once again that we are reading Nick's interpretation, filtered through his defective vision. Finally, sprawled out on the beach, he broods 'on the old, unknown world', trying to see through the eyes of the pioneering Dutch sailors.

hyperbole: deliberate exaggeration for effect.

Build critical skills

Nick interprets the scene through the pantry window as revealing 'intimacy' between Tom and Daisy, that they are 'conspiring together'. Could the fact that Tom's hand 'covers' Daisy's suggests a different interpretation?

Windows

Fitzgerald increases the mystery and ambiguity surrounding events through numerous references to windows, in which the observer's vision may have been distorted. Fitzgerald seems to be warning his readers to mistrust the perceptions of his narrator, who thinks **'life is much more successfully looked at from a single window'**.

Top ten quotation

In some references the observers' understanding of what they see is definitely imaginary. Looking through the window of Gatsby's house, Daisy thinks the clouds look solid enough to support Gatsby's weight. Daisy romantically assumes she can keep Gatsby as a sort of doll, to play with when she wants to. Myrtle looks out of a window at the garage and sees Tom with another woman. However, what appears to be the truth that the other woman is his wife or a new mistress is actually an illusion.

Wilson looks through the window at the faded advertisement for Dr T.J. Eckleburg and believes that the eyes belong to God, but these eyes are blind.

Wilson is taken in by the appearance, but the reader understands the reality. While the people who live in the valley of ashes are losing their dreams and dying, turning into ash or dust, Dr T.J. Eckleburg will ironically live on and survive to represent the age of materialism.

Religion

Fitzgerald had a strongly religious, Catholic upbringing, and there is a powerful spiritual element at work in this novel. He exposes the emptiness beneath the glittering sophistication of post-war America, and he invokes religion to demonstrate it.

The most explicitly religious reference comes when Wilson looks at the eyes of Dr T.J. Eckleburg and tells Michaelis how he told Myrtle: 'God knows what you've been doing, everything you've been doing. You may fool me, but you can't fool God!' The fact that Wilson equates an advertisement with God suggests that spiritual values have been replaced by empty, meaningless images.

There are several references directly linking Gatsby with Christianity. He claims that what he tells Nick about his past is 'God's truth' and 'his right hand suddenly ordered divine retribution to stand by' (p. 63). However, everything he tells Nick is either an obvious lie or is disproved later in the novel. Nick claims 'He was a son of God … and he must be about His Father's business, the service of a vast, vulgar and meretricious beauty' (p. 95). Fitzgerald's use of capitalisation and the fact that the phrases are taken **verbatim** from the Bible clearly signal that he wants to link Gatsby with Christ. This reference, however, must be ironic. His adopted father is Cody, an unscrupulous self-made millionaire, so 'His Father's business' must be amassing a fortune by any means.

Nick says that Gatsby 'knew that when he kissed this girl, and forever wed his unutterable visions to her perishable breath, his mind would never romp again like the mind of God' (p. 107). This suggests that this was the moment when Gatsby abandoned his lofty ambitions in order to pursue wealth so that he could win Daisy. If that is what Nick means, then Fitzgerald has shown us that Nick is mistaken, as Gatsby had already dedicated himself to the pursuit of worldly wealth before he met Daisy, when he changed his name and rowed out to Cody's yacht.

Context

Six months after the publication of *The Great Gatsby*, Fitzgerald wrote in a letter that young people in America are 'brave, shallow, cynical, impatient, turbulent and empty. I like them not.' (from a letter written by Fitzgerald to Marya Mannes in 1925 (full URL on p.102)).

verbatim: in exactly the same words.

CRITICAL VIEW

'In expressing these feelings – the feeling that life is unendurable without a belief in the possibility of a meaningful existence, and the feeling that the world conspires to make such a belief impossible – Fitzgerald spoke for his own time and perhaps, in a broader sense, for all generations of Americans – as the ending of *The Great Gatsby*, with its overt reference to our American past, suggests he himself felt.'
(Arthur Mizener, introduction to *Twentieth Century Views*, 1963)

St John's Gospel says that Christ carried his own cross. Christ died at the 'ninth hour' of daylight, i.e. three o'clock in the afternoon, and that he rose 'on the third day'. Gatsby 'shouldered the mattress', died in the middle of the afternoon, and 'on the third day' came a telegram from his father and Gatsby's true identity was revealed. Of course, these echoes of the Crucifixion may be accidental, but in an examination they could still gain credit for connections with other texts.

Nevertheless, these religious references say more about the narrator than they do about the eponymous hero. Although Nick clearly had a religious upbringing and has a strong moral code, it seems that he no longer believes in God. He appears to be searching for something to fill that spiritual need in his life when he meets Gatsby. What attracts him to Gatsby is his 'extraordinary gift for hope, a romantic readiness'. Like Christ, Gatsby offers the promise of something better, **'the orgastic future that year by year recedes before us'**.

> **Top ten quotation**

The seven deadly sins

Further evidence of Nick's religious training can be found in his illustrations of the seven deadly sins. Tom speaks with **pride** about being a member of the 'dominant race' and asserts that it is up to them to watch out 'or these other races will have control of things'. This reveals that the American Dream is not open to all, as Americans of North European origin work to keep power for themselves.

Fitzgerald exposes a materialistic society based on **envy** when he reveals that Gatsby's pursuit of Daisy originally sprang from a desire to take her 'because he had no real right to touch her hand' (p. 142).

> **TASK**
> Find evidence for each of the other sins in The Great Gatsby: Gluttony, Lust, Avarice, Wrath and Sloth.

The seven cardinal virtues

Fitzgerald also demonstrates that the post-war generation has subverted the cardinal virtues to the point where they have become their opposite. The religious roots of the dream of the original Puritan settlers and the Founding Fathers were corrupted from the start by commercial exploitation, and Fitzgerald seems to feel that, by the 1920s, materialism has completely taken over people's lives.

Nick observes that 'everyone suspects himself of at least one of the cardinal virtues' (p. 59) and claims that his virtue is honesty; however, he lies to the girl back home and misleads the girl in the office as well as Jordan. He seems to think that, as long as he breaks off relationships 'tactfully', he is still being honest by the standards he sets for other men. He seems to equate honesty with **prudence**, as he manages to disentangle himself from relationships and commit himself to nothing. However, the fact that, at the age of 30, he is still financially dependent on his father and has no plans for the future suggests that his is not the prudence advocated by the Founding Fathers.

> **TASK**
> Explore the novel for evidence of each of the virtues: Prudence, Faith, Hope, Love, Justice, Fortitude, Temperance.

When Nick learns that Wolfshiem was responsible for fixing the Baseball World Series, he admits that 'It never occurred to me that one man could start to play with the faith of fifty million people.' Fitzgerald's use of the word 'faith' here

Top ten quotation

Mammon: 'wealth' or material possessions, a false object of worship and devotion.

is ironic, as God has been replaced by sport and the desire to make money by betting on its outcome. On Sunday mornings, '**the world and its mistress returned to Gatsby's house**'; this society worships **Mammon**, not God.

The post-war generation seems to have abandoned the cardinal virtues, except for Gatsby, but his **faith**, **hope** and **love** are misdirected into trying to recreate the past and persuade another man's wife to declare her love for him and abandon her child.

'The World's Fair'

▲ Gatsby's house in the 2013 Baz Luhrmann film

metaphor: a suppressed comparison which is implied but not stated.

Nick tells Gatsby that his place looks like 'the World's Fair', and he is clearly tapping into a well-known literary concept. Since *The Pilgrim's Progress* was published in 1678, the concept of society being a 'fair' has frequently been employed by writers. W.M. Thackeray clearly explains this **metaphor** in his novel *Vanity Fair* (1847): 'Vanity Fair is a very vain, wicked, foolish place, full of all sorts of humbugs and falsenesses and pretensions'.

Context

In *The Pilgrim's Progress*, John Bunyan describes a place called Vanity Fair that offers his hero worldly pleasures to tempt him away from his pilgrimage to the Celestial City. His allegorical character, Faithful, is killed by the people of Vanity Fair in a clear accusation that people who succumb to vanity, putting wealth, property and status in society above everything else, lose all the cardinal virtues.

Fitzgerald initially intended his short story, 'Absolution', to be the prologue to *The Great Gatsby*, giving insights into his eponymous hero's upbringing. In this story, the priest tells the boy to go to see a 'glittering' amusement park, but to not get too close 'because if you do you'll only feel the heat and the sweat and the life'. The boy sits there, half-terrified, 'but underneath his terror he felt that … There was something ineffably gorgeous somewhere that had nothing to do with God.'

In the epigraph, Fitzgerald suggests that Gatsby has to act like a circus performer and become the 'gold-hatted, high-bouncing lover' in order to win Daisy.

At Gatsby's parties, there are 'enough coloured lights to make a Christmas tree of Gatsby's enormous garden', and the guests 'conducted themselves according to the rules of behaviour associated with an amusement park'. However, when he meets Daisy again, Gatsby's 'career as Trimalchio was over'; Nick notes that 'the whole caravansary had fallen in like a card house at the disapproval in her eyes' (p. 109).

From this point on, Nick no longer uses the language of the fairground, he seems obsessed with 'the heat and the sweat'. Nick was attracted to the gorgeous World's Fair, but he is aware of its falseness, and the description of his underwear as 'a snake' reinforces the idea of temptation and betrayal. Like the boy in *Absolution*, he has realised at last that what appears 'ineffably gorgeous' has 'nothing to do with God'. By the last chapter, he has realised that the American Dream is the 'orgastic future that year by year recedes before us'.

Gender roles

The Great War had the most significant impact on women's roles. During the war, women had become used to filling men's roles in the workplace; they had more freedom and financial independence. The Nineteenth Amendment of 1920 gave women the right to vote. More women were going to university and seeking fulfilment outside the home. The rapid growth in mass-produced cars gave them the opportunity for greater mobility, and new technology created celebrities in entertainment and in sport. The original wording of the Declaration of Independence promised the Dream to men, but, in the Roaring Twenties, it became possible for women to pursue it. Some people, however, thought that this went 'against Nature' and would be injurious to women's physical and mental health, particularly their fertility.

Jordan

Jordan Baker, named after two automobile manufacturers, epitomises the New Woman. She was based on Edith Cummings, a well-known professional golfer, whom Fitzgerald knew when he was a student at Princeton University. She seems to have achieved the American Dream, having achieved success and

Taking it further

Read Fitzgerald's short story 'Absolution' and explore how you could use this as a comparative text in an essay on the aspects of tragedy: www.gutenberg. net.au/fsf/ABSOLUTION. html

Build critical skills

The epigraph is attributed to Thomas Parke D'Invilliers. However, he was a fictional character in Fitzgerald's *This Side of Paradise*. What does the epigraph suggest about Fitzgerald's attitude towards Daisy? (See p.61 for more information.)

independence through her own hard work. However, her success does not bring her 'happiness'. She is the target of possibly unfounded accusations of cheating, which Nick spreads, and men pursue her, not for herself, but in order to share in her fame.

▲ Edith Cummings on the cover of *Time* magazine

Daisy

Before marriage, Daisy had her own car and worked voluntarily for the Red Cross. However, Daisy grew up in the old-fashioned world of Kentucky, and she belongs to a class in which women were not expected to support themselves. Marriage was the only appropriate way for her to break away from parental control. As a married woman, Daisy has less freedom than in her youth as she has no car of her own.

Myrtle

Myrtle is poor, and the war has had little impact on her opportunities. She has aspirations to raise herself into a higher class, but she has neither the education nor the talent to do this on her own. This means that she can only pull herself out of the valley of ashes with the help of a man, like Tom Buchanan.

Target your thinking

- How far does the reader's response to Nick Carraway colour their perception of the other characters? (**AO1**)
- How has Fitzgerald helped his readers to understand his characters by giving them each a distinctive way of speaking? (**AO2**)
- Where do you stand in the debate about Daisy? Is she an innocent romantic or an unscrupulous betrayer? (**AO5**)

Jay Gatsby

The eponymous hero was born James Gatz, the son of farmers in the Midwest. He left home at around 16 and changed his name when he joined Dan Cody. Nick describes Cody as 'James Gatz's destiny', and from Cody he received a 'singularly appropriate education'. Gatsby met Daisy while at training camp, when his poor background was disguised by an officer's uniform, and they had a brief but passionate affair.

◀ Gatsby, the 'elegant young rough-neck'

Build critical skills

Re-read the first three pages of Chapter VIII, and analyse Nick's use of words like 'value', 'took', 'ravenously' and 'unscrupulously'. Explore how Nick's choice of language reveals the influence of Cody on the nature of Gatsby's feelings for Daisy.

Taking it further ▶▶

Research the story of the Holy Grail and explain what its use here tells the reader about Nick and his fascination with Gatsby.

CRITICAL VIEW

'The worst fault in [*The Great Gatsby*] I think is a BIG FAULT: I gave no account (and had no feeling about or knowledge of) the emotional relations between Gatsby and Daisy from the time of their reunion to the catastrophe.' (Fitzgerald to Edmund Wilson, 1925)

Gatsby fought in the Great War and, on his return, went to New York to make his fortune. He claims that this was so that he would be in the same circle as Daisy, because he hoped to recreate the past. However, the house is conveniently situated on the tip of Long Island, where he could land smuggled alcohol. Fitzgerald uses an unreliable narrator to present Gatsby as a mysterious character, fabulously wealthy, who throws lavish parties in the hopes of meeting Daisy. Nick sees Gatsby as a romantic idealist who engages in criminal activities to fund the pursuit of his dream. Gatsby uses Nick to gain an introduction to Daisy, and he deliberately feeds Nick's romantic imagination.

Fitzgerald introduces this man of mystery through hints such as Daisy's reaction to his name in Chapter I, and rumours: that he is 'a nephew or a cousin of Kaiser Wilhelm's'; 'he doesn't want any trouble with ANYbody'; 'he killed a man once'; 'he was a German spy during the war'; 'he grew up … in Germany'. Nick reports all the gossip about Gatsby, but he thinks of it as 'babbled slander', and describes it as 'romantic speculation'; it seems to increase his fascination with the mysterious Gatsby. Nick is seduced by Gatsby's smile, which gives the impression of a man of rare charm who makes Nick feel special.

▲ Gatsby's 'rare' smile 'with a quality of eternal reassurance in it': Robert Redford in the 1974 Jack Clayton film

When he stops smiling, Nick perceives an uncultured but ultra-polite young man who speaks with studied formality to conceal his origins, but sometimes Gatsby's mask slips, giving Nick a glimpse of the hard man at the heart of the romantic dreamer.

At times, Gatsby almost gives the game away, as when 'He hurried the phrase "educated at Oxford", or swallowed it, or choked on it', as if he is laughing at Nick's gullibility. Gatsby soon recovers, however, and makes extravagant claims about his war experiences. He shows Nick a medal and a photograph, and Nick's reaction is extreme; he is totally persuaded about 'the gnawings of his broken heart'. Gatsby seems to be cleverly manipulating Nick, so that, when Jordan asks Nick to arrange a secret rendezvous for Gatsby with another man's wife, he is surprised at 'the modesty of the demand'.

Gatsby repeatedly calls all the men he meets by the unfashionable epithet 'old sport'. He uses no figurative language and no complex syntax, often lapsing into incomplete utterances. He uses a lot of clichés such as 'lived like a young rajah', 'trying to forget something very sad that had happened to me long ago', 'I tried very hard to die, but I seemed to bear an enchanted life'. Gatsby lacks the vocabulary to express his thoughts, telling Daisy 'I keep it always full of interesting people, night and day. People who do interesting things. Celebrated people.' Fitzgerald uses **aposiopesis** to make him sound inarticulate, for instance, when Daisy uses his hairbrush, he says to Nick, 'It's the funniest thing, old sport … I can't— When I try to—'.

Nick clearly admires Gatsby for being a faithful lover, even after the object of his love marries someone else. He chivalrously intends to take the blame when Daisy kills Myrtle, and he keeps a sacred 'vigil' that night to protect Daisy. However, Fitzgerald may be calling him 'Great' ironically, linking him with circus performers and showmen like Phineas T. Barnum who advertised their acts as 'Great'. It is surely ironic that the one apparently chivalrous character in the novel is engaged in business that is intended to cheat and defraud.

Throughout the novel there are mysterious telephone calls and other hints that Gatsby is involved in shady activities, some of which, as he tells Nick when he offers him 'a little business on the side', have nothing to do with Wolfshiem. It is not until after Gatsby is killed and Nick answers his telephone that the mystery is partly resolved. Unaware that he is talking to the wrong person, the caller blurts out that the police arrested 'Young Parke' when he handed stolen security bonds over the counter. 'They got a circular from New York giving 'em the numbers just five minutes before.'

Nick Carraway

Nick Carraway is the novel's narrator, and we see all the other characters from his point of view. He has a unique perspective because he is '**within and without, simultaneously enchanted and repelled by the inexhaustible variety of life**'.

He comes from a wealthy family and is ignorant of the poverty of many in New York. In the valley of ashes, Nick cannot believe people live in such conditions, so he thinks that the garage must be a 'blind and that sumptuous and romantic apartments were concealed overhead'. He has entry into the society of the rich residents of East Egg because of his kinship with Daisy, but he is not part of their world.

He was brought up in the Midwest, graduated from Yale University and fought in the Great War. When he returned, he could not settle back into a place with such a narrow perspective on life. His father is funding his year in New York to learn the bond business. He rents a cottage on West Egg, next to Gatsby's

Taking it further ▶

Watch Baz Luhrmann's 2013 film of *The Great Gatsby*. How does the director make the viewer aware of the sinister side of Gatsby?

aposiopesis: incomplete utterance caused by emotion or confusion.

CRITICAL VIEW

'Like Willy Loman, Gatsby has all the wrong dreams but the single-mindedness, the spiritual integrity with which he pursues them, commands respect.' (C.W.E. Bigsby, 'The Two Identities of F. Scott Fitzgerald', from *The American Novel and the 1920s*, 1971)

Top ten quotation

mansion, and he makes it possible for Gatsby to meet Daisy. Nick dreams of romance, but is unable to commit himself, and seems to have settled for a dream of wealth. However, he does not work at this; the dozen books he buys remain on the shelf, only 'promising to unfold the shining secrets'.

Nick is snobbish, boasting of being 'descended from the Dukes of Buccleuch' and speaking disparagingly of the 'demoniac Finn' who is his housekeeper. He has had a puritanical upbringing that has erroneously taught him that 'a sense of the fundamental decencies is parcelled out unequally at birth', so, in spite of boasting of his tolerance, he is quick to judge others. However, the man who condemns Jordan as 'incurably dishonest' and claims to be 'one of the few honest people' he has ever known, also lies to the girl back home and thinks that being asked to help Gatsby to seduce another man's wife is a 'modest' demand, 'such a little thing'.

He seems to be unable to commit himself to anyone, but his romantic soul admires Gatsby's obsession and seems to think love excuses everything. He is not merely a bystander but complicit in the seduction. He tells Daisy not to bring Tom when he invites her to meet Gatsby, and, to give Gatsby and Daisy privacy, Nick leaves the room and stands outside in the rain. Once again, in Chapter VI, he 'remained watchfully in the garden' while Gatsby and Daisy go to his house to be alone.

Build critical skills

Near the end of Chapter IV, Nick writes that, as he listened to Jordan's story, Gatsby 'came alive' to him. From this point on, Nick is committed to Gatsby. What is it that brings about this change of heart in the narrator and how significant is it?

CRITICAL VIEW

A psychoanalytic critic would judge that Nick has a highly developed super-ego, and so his upbringing leads him to disapprove of all the other characters. However, his id, representing his inner desires, encourages him to forgive Gatsby, excusing his dishonesty because he admires, and perhaps envies, Gatsby's romantic vision.

To Nick, the romantic potential of any object depends on its inaccessibility, so, even at the first meeting between Daisy and Gatsby, Nick imagines that Daisy has 'tumbled short of his dreams' because she is no longer out of reach. At the end, when Gatsby is floating on the pool, Nick imagines that he is waiting for a phone call from Daisy that he 'didn't believe' would come. Nick's desire for a romantic ending to the story and his prejudice against women blind him to his knowledge that Gatsby's telephone line was blocked to keep it open for a business call.

Nick supposedly took time crafting his narrative. He started writing the book in 1923, as he refers to coming back from the East 'last autumn' (Chapter I), and finished it in 1924, 'after two years' (Chapter IX). Fitzgerald gives his narrator a distinctive voice, using the Latinate vocabulary one might expect from a graduate of Yale, but also using **colloquial language** that conveys informality; we often feel he is talking to us rather than crafting a book. However, he rarely uses sophisticated polysyllabic words in speech. He uses colloquialisms and occasionally swearwords to express intense emotion: 'They're a rotten crowd … You're worth the whole damn bunch put together.' He is also able to slip easily into Daisy's hyperbolic and inconsequential style of chatter.

colloquial language: informal language of conversational speech.

CRITICAL VIEW

Judith Fetterley, a feminist critic, wrote: 'Nick's dishonesty goes unrecognised by most of the novel's readers: it is not perceived as dishonest because it is common, pervasive, and "natural" to a sexist society. *The Great Gatsby* is a dishonest book because the culture from which it derives and which it reflects is radically dishonest.'
(Judith Fetterley, *The Resisting Reader: A Feminist Approach to American Fiction*, 1977)

Build critical skills

Why do you think Nick does not tell what he knows at the inquest?

Daisy Buchanan (née Fay)

CRITICAL VIEW

'… the golden girl is revealed to be a common weed …'
'Women are the object of the novel's moral indignation just as they are the object of its romanticism.'
(Judith Fetterley, *The Resisting Reader: A Feminist Approach to American Fiction*, 1977)

▲ Daisy has pure, unaffected innocence underneath her cynicism: Carey Mulligan in the 2013 Baz Luhrmann film

The derivation of the flower's name is from the phrase 'day's eye', and Daisy certainly glows like the sun. However, a daisy is a surprising flower to choose as the name for the rich, sophisticated woman whom Gatsby loves so obsessively. It certainly does not suggest wealth or even beauty, but perhaps Fitzgerald wished to suggest that she retained a pure, unaffected innocence underneath her cynicism. She is still the nice girl who grew up in Louisville, immaculately dressed in white and lamenting her white girlhood.

'Fay' is an archaic word for fairy, and, according to Nick, Gatsby's perception of Daisy is one of enchantment. He is 'consumed with wonder at her presence', and, when he first kissed her, 'At his lips' touch she blossomed for him like a flower and the incarnation was complete'. However, in the Arthurian legends, Morgan le Fay is a seductive sorceress who uses her magical powers to

Taking it further ▶

When you have watched one of the films, consider how successfully the enigma of Daisy's character has been portrayed.

TASK

Look beneath Nick's superficial judgements, and note down what impression of Daisy we can gain from Nick's first visit.

Build critical skills

Nick complains 'without resentment, that Daisy hadn't sent a message or a flower'. Can you find any evidence that Nick is correct to assume that Daisy knew about Gatsby's death before the funeral?

CRITICAL VIEW

'If the book fails commercially it will be from one of two reasons or both. First, the title is only fair, rather bad than good. Second and most important, the book contains no important woman character.' (Fitzgerald to Maxwell Perkins, 1925)

try to overthrow Arthur. Daisy Fay's name encapsulates the enigma of the character, and readers are left to make up their own minds whether she is the innocent girl of Gatsby's dream, or a seductive sorceress, using him and then betraying him.

In the novel's present, Daisy is 23, disillusioned and unhappy because of her husband's infidelity. However, she hides her feelings behind a mask of shallow cynicism. Just a few years earlier she had been the 'golden girl' with everything before her, but now, thanks to Tom's 'little spree' in Chicago, she is living in relative isolation in East Egg, and Jordan thinks 'Daisy ought to have something in her life'.

Context

Louisville is in Kentucky, one of the Southern States. Scottie, Fitzgerald's daughter, criticised Mia Farrow's portrayal of Daisy in the 1974 film because she did not convey the 'intensely Southern' nature of Daisy's character.

Daisy wants to show off her baby to her cousin, but Nick thinks this desire is 'irrelevant', and Tom interrupts her. She puts on an act of helplessness, stuttering a little and using hyperbole. She uses a lot of short questions, exclamations, empty adjectives such as 'gorgeous' and 'absolute' and tells empty stories like the one about the butler's nose. She appears to be talking just to be sociable and to create a light-hearted atmosphere, not because she has anything meaningful to say. When she is alone with Nick, she uses a more direct style of speech as she tries to confide in him, but he is unreceptive, assuming that she is still indulging in sociable chatter. Because the narrator has judged her to be insincere, and Fitzgerald never gives her an opportunity to speak for herself, the reader never gets the chance to understand Daisy.

Tom Buchanan

Tom's wealth is inherited, placing him socially in the old-established 'aristocracy'. Apparently a successful achiever of the American Dream, Tom has not achieved his wealth through his own efforts and he is linked with ruthless exploitation, as Chicago had a notorious meat-packing industry with an appalling record of abusing the workers (see the **Context** box on p.41). He was educated at Yale University, where he distinguished himself on the football field, and he still has the physique of an American football player. He is now a well-known polo player, and his muscles strain against the riding clothes he wears. Like his clothes, his veneer of civilised behaviour has difficulty keeping his strength under control. He is domineering, aggressive and arrogant.

CRITICAL VIEW

' … the characters are not "developed": the wealthy and brutal Tom Buchanan haunted by his "scientific" vision of the doom of civilisation, the vaguely guilty, vaguely homosexual Jordan Baker, the dim Wolfshiem, who fixed the World Series of 1919, are treated, we might say, as if they were ideographs, a method of economy that is reinforced by the ideographic use that is made of the Washington Heights' flat, the terrible "valley of ashes" seen from the Long Island Railroad, Gatsby's incoherent parties, and the huge sordid eyes of the oculist's advertising sign.'
(Lionel Trilling, *The Liberal Imagination*, 1950)

Tom has had a succession of affairs in the three years since his marriage and is keen to show off his current mistress, but he claims that 'in my heart I love her [Daisy] all the time'. He is blatantly hypocritical, being outraged at Daisy's relationship with Gatsby. The most unpleasant thing about him is his self-righteousness and self-absorption. Tom has a hierarchical view of society with him and his ilk at the top, and he violently disapproves of anything that threatens his superiority. He is an extreme racist, although he does not have the intelligence to understand the book he has been reading, and he disapproves of women having too much freedom.

Taking it further ▶▶

Jordan tells Nick that Tom took Daisy away from Chicago after he was involved in a scandal. Significantly, Daisy came out with 'an absolutely perfect reputation'. Do some further research into Chicago in the 1920s and explore why such a rich man might have had to move from Chicago, and why he might have chosen to move to a house on the very tip of East Egg, in Long Island Sound.

Tom feels justified in giving Wilson directions to Gatsby's house, even though Wilson has a gun. Although he claims the moral high ground in the confrontation with Gatsby, he is not untouched by corruption. He is friendly with Walter Chase (one of Wolfshiem's and Gatsby's criminal associates), he frequents speakeasies, (see the **Context** box on p.42) like the one in the cellar on Forty-Second Street, he buys alcohol illegally and even smuggles it into the Plaza Hotel. He may even smuggle alcohol into the country via the strategic position of his house. Tom is both amoral and ruthless. When he breaks Myrtle's nose, he does not even take her to hospital.

Tom's first word is the first person singular subject pronoun. The declaration he makes, 'I've got a nice place here', excludes his wife, suggesting egocentrism and arrogance. He speaks assertively and 'violently' (e.g. 'Civilisation's going to pieces'), but his authority is undermined by his use of vague, **basic speaking vocabulary** (e.g. 'It's all scientific stuff' and 'science and art, and all that'). He speaks aggressively, using swearwords ('God damned fool'), and with women

Context

Upton Sinclair exposed corruption in the Chicago meat-packing industry in his novel *The Jungle* (1906). Ironically, instead of horrifying people at the situation of the workers, who sometimes fell into the meat-processing tanks and were ground up along with the meat, his novel provoked an outcry against the lack of food-safety measures, highlighting even further the hypocrisy of society.

basic speaking vocabulary: vague words that are used in everyday speech, but usually replaced with a more precise term in writing, e.g. 'stuff', 'a lot'.

he violates the rules of turn-taking by interrupting both Daisy and Jordan, but not Nick.

Jordan Baker

As a well-known sports celebrity and 'New Woman', Jordan seems to have achieved the American Dream at the age of 21. At 16, she thought that the best thing for Daisy was to marry the wealthy, good-looking Tom Buchanan, and she literally forced her to marry him when a letter from Gatsby changed Daisy's mind. Five years later she is disillusioned and thinks that 'Daisy ought to have something in her life', so she persuades Nick to invite Daisy to meet Gatsby behind Tom's back.

Nick calls her a 'clean, hard, limited person, who dealt in universal scepticism', and Fitzgerald shows that achieving the Dream does not necessarily bring happiness. Jordan has no family except an elderly aunt, so she has had to learn to look out for herself. She needs to protect herself from all the flattering young men, attracted to her because of her sporting success, and she is the target of nasty gossip. She has adopted a pose of contemptuous cynicism and self-sufficiency which Nick finds intimidating.

Unlike Daisy, Jordan says very little and seems to weigh her words carefully. She can engage in this sociable 'bantering inconsequence', but she usually uses a more assertive manner of speaking than Daisy, reflecting her independent, sporty image. Her first word 'Absolutely' expresses a vehement agreement that Tom should stay in the East. Whereas Daisy uses the adjectival form without meaning in phrases like 'an absolute rose', Jordan uses the adverb to be assertive. Her first words to Nick, 'You live in West Egg', are a declarative statement, issued rather like a challenge, and, since he is not used to forthright women, he interprets her tone as contemptuous. She issues commands to Nick, 'Don't talk', and takes control of the conversation. Although she ignores him when he arrives, she says 'Good night, Mr Carraway. See you anon', leaving the possibility open for another meeting.

When Daisy and Tom are arguing about the phone call, Jordan 'leaned forward unashamed, trying to hear'. Nick assumes that she is revealing an unpleasant interest, but she probably simply wants to protect her friend. She might be feeling guilty at forcing Daisy to marry this philanderer. It may be that she agrees to act as go-between for Gatsby because she wants to make it up to her friend.

After Myrtle's death, Jordan swallows her pride and twice asks Nick to come into the house. When she telephones him the following day, her voice, which was usually fresh and cool, 'seemed harsh and dry over the phone'.

She gives him an opportunity to make amends for his behaviour, but his insensitive reply leaves her silent, perhaps wondering how to express her need for him without appearing vulnerable. She phrases her request in the most straightforward way, 'I want to see you', so that he does not know how hurt she is. She even offers to cancel her plans.

When Nick ends his relationship with her, he talks nervously while she lies perfectly still listening. Once again, her chin is 'raised a little jauntily', and the reader recognises the familiar sign that she is adopting a mask. She has planned her defensive strategy, telling him she is engaged to another man. However, she suddenly blurts out how much he hurt her. She says 'I don't give a damn about you now', the adverb revealing that she did care for him then. She accuses him of not being honest and straightforward, as he pretends, but refuses to allow herself to be dragged into an argument. She has let her guard down a little, enough to make him 'angry', but retained her dignity. Nick feels threatened by her poise, her detachment, her independence.

Myrtle Wilson

Myrtle is Tom's current lover. Unlike the delicate daisy, myrtle is a hardy evergreen shrub which was sacred to Aphrodite, Greek goddess of love. Like her namesake, Myrtle is vigorous and manages to retain her lust for life even after twelve years living in the valley of ashes. Nick says 'there was an immediately perceptible vitality about her as if the nerves of her body were continually smouldering'. It is this vitality which refuses to let her give up as her husband has done, which makes her grasp at the chance to lift herself out of poverty and which sends her out into the road in front of the car, refusing to give up her dream of a better life.

Like Gatsby, Myrtle has a strong dream; however she can only achieve it through a man. She has been married twelve years and has no children. Tom seems to offer the only chance she will have to change her life before she too becomes one of the ash-grey inhabitants of the waste land. Having, as she thinks, lifted herself out of the spiritless, hopeless environs of the valley of ashes, she despises her husband and speaks with contempt of her own class. However, her dream is built on the lie that Tom would marry her if he could divorce Daisy, but he claims that she is Catholic.

Nick sneers at Myrtle's attempts to lift herself into a higher social stratum. He mocks her movements and her voice. He even employs non-standard **orthography** to mock her lower-class accent with 'you'd of thought' and 'appendicitus'. This undermines her pretensions to belong to the moneyed class who employ servants. She uses clumsy grammatical constructions like the multiple negative, 'I didn't hardly know I wasn't getting into a subway train' (p. 38). She uses a basic speaking vocabulary without auxiliary verbs, 'I *got* to write down a list so I won't forget all the things I *got* to do'.

Fitzgerald describes Myrtle in detail after the accident, and he insisted to his publisher that he did not want to change the wording.

NB for a detailed analysis of this description, turn to **Building skills 2: Analysing texts in detail** on page 92.

Build critical skills

Why do you think Fitzgerald did not want Nick to stay to help when Tom breaks Myrtle's nose, but has him take advantage of the confusion to slip out with Mr McKee?

CRITICAL VIEW

'I'm sorry Myrtle is better than Daisy … It's Chapter VII that's the trouble with Daisy and it may hurt the book's popularity that it's a man's book.' (Fitzgerald to Maxwell Perkins, 1925) Do you think Fitzgerald was right to be pleased with his presentation of Myrtle?

Orthography: the term used for accepted spelling.

George Wilson

Wilson runs a garage, but the single wrecked car in it is covered in dust, suggesting he is too tired to work, or even to dream. At first glance, Nick describes Wilson as a 'blond, spiritless man, anaemic, and faintly handsome'. His neighbour, Michaelis, says that 'generally he was one of those worn-out men: when he wasn't working, he sat on a chair in the doorway and stared at the people and cars that passed along the road … He was his wife's man and not his own.' Michaelis 'was almost sure that Wilson had no friend: there was not enough of him for his wife'.

However, he clearly loves Myrtle. When he learns about Myrtle's affair, he acts decisively, locking her in an upstairs room and setting about finding the money to take her West. His love for Myrtle gives him the strength to act. When she is killed, Wilson is distraught, but a mere twelve hours or so later he sets off to find the driver of the car that killed her. He walks to the tip of East Egg and then Tom sends him to Gatsby's house. Wilson then walks all the way back down East Egg and up to the tip of West Egg. Having been told that Gatsby's car killed Myrtle, he assumed that Gatsby was her lover because she recognised the car and ran out to speak to the driver.

Wilson dies at the scene of Gatsby's death, but Fitzgerald gives his readers no details about the gun or the manner of his death, leaving the deaths a mystery. George Wilson is the one who gets the blame for Gatsby's death and then his own. Nick reports that 'Wilson was reduced to a man "deranged by grief" in order that the case might remain in its simplest form', suggesting that he did not believe that the inquest had returned a true verdict. However, he fails to tell what he knows.

Meyer Wolfshiem

Meyer Wolfshiem's name brands him a predator, and his cufflinks, made from human molars, suggest sinister associations. He is a ruthless gangster, supposedly responsible for fixing the Baseball World Series in 1919 and involved in a range of other illegal activities, including blatant and very lucrative 'over the counter' sales of illegal alcohol. Wolfshiem scared Walter Chase into 'shutting his mouth' and not informing against him and Gatsby for breaking betting laws. Now, they are into something bigger which Chase is too scared to talk about.

Fitzgerald sets Wolfshiem firmly in the contemporary criminal fraternity by linking him with Herman Rosenthal, a real gambler who was gunned down by the police. Wolfshiem himself reveals that he uses a thug, Katspaugh, to silence the opposition. Wolfshiem recruited Gatsby when the latter returned from the war because he realised he 'could use him good', and he claims that they were closely involved in everything, 'always together'. However, he refuses to go to Gatsby's funeral, not wanting to 'get mixed up in it in any way'.

Build critical skills

When Gatsby starts his affair with Daisy, he dismisses all his servants and replaces them with 'some people Wolfshiem wanted to do something for'. Why do you think Fitzgerald makes a point of saying in Nick's description of the day Gatsby died that the chauffeur who heard the shots but did nothing was 'one of Wolfshiem's protégés'?

Gatsby's powerful and ruthless business associate seems to be a recent immigrant, speaking English with a marked accent and non-standard grammar. Nick's mocking anti-Semitism means that Wolfshiem actually comes across as quite a comic character with his 'tragic nose' and the quivering hair in his nostrils (p. 163). Fitzgerald seems to be suggesting that Nick's snobbery makes him underestimate Wolfshiem.

NB for analysis of Wolfshiem's idiolect, see **Writer's methods: Dramatist** on pages 51–2.

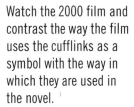

Taking it further

Watch the 2000 film and contrast the way the film uses the cufflinks as a symbol with the way in which they are used in the novel.

Writer's methods: Form, structure and language

Target your thinking

- Consider the authorial methods – such as symbolism and narrative viewpoint – that Fitzgerald uses. Which do you feel are the three most important and how is each used to shape meaning and to create effects? **(AO2)**
- What is the significance of the fact that each of the settings is firmly based in a contemporary context? **(AO3)**
- What other text have you studied in which the writer's use of a first person narrator makes it difficult to work out the truth about what happens? **(AO4)**

Viewpoint

In a first person narrative, an understanding of the character who is selected to put their own version of events foward is crucial to an understanding of the whole novel. When the narrator is also a character who is involved in events as well as commenting on them, readers need to be alert and prepared to question the accuracy of his account.

Fitzgerald has chosen a narrator who is only partially involved, so at times he has to use the testimony of other characters. However, Nick's unreliability leads us to question his account of what he claims others have told him, so different interpretations of events are possible. This means that key scenes of the story can be left to the reader's imagination, thus enhancing the mystery. Fitzgerald's choice of narrator allows us to glimpse the glory of Gatsby's illusion and simultaneously makes us aware of its hopelessness by keeping us in touch with reality.

Nick is judgemental and talks about his fellow Americans as if he were an outsider: 'Americans, while willing, even eager, to be serfs, have always been obstinate about being peasantry.' He has a vivid imagination that he uses to interpret people's reactions and feelings, but this makes him gullible. This means that Fitzgerald can gloss over the means by which Gatsby became rich and concentrate on his dream instead. Fitzgerald reveals that Nick longs for romance, something to give a purpose to his life. The original dust jacket for the novel depicted this 'disembodied face' which 'floated along dark cornices and blinding signs' (p. 78), putting this longing of Nick's at the heart of the book. The way he presents the other characters is influenced by his unfulfilled desire. Furthermore, Nick has had limited experience of life, which may lead him to misinterpret events (see **Characters**, pages 37–8). Nick's upbringing allows Fitzgerald to reveal his own feelings about the hollowness of the lives of the post-war generation.

> Top ten quotation

Self-conscious narrator

Nick prides himself on having been 'rather literary in college', and Fitzgerald establishes that Nick is self-consciously crafting his narrative. We know from page 8 that Nick started writing the year following his return from the East, and, on page 155, at the beginning of the final chapter, he tells us it is two years since Gatsby died. He supposedly takes a year to fashion the story in the way in which he wants his readers to receive it.

Literary devices

With his literary aspirations, Nick often uses metaphors. Gatsby, for instance, is portrayed as a victim through Fitzgerald's use of a metaphor evoking predatory wild animals; it is not Gatsby himself who has disillusioned Nick, but 'what preyed on Gatsby'.

The fascination with Gatsby

Gatsby promised to tell Nick 'God's truth' (p. 65), and then he tells the stupid and obvious lie that he was brought up in the Middle West, in San Francisco. At first Nick is, understandably, 'incredulous', then fascinated by Gatsby's claims, and then he appears to be finally convinced by a photograph and a medal. In this passage, Nick's relief is ludicrously exaggerated, as he claims to see Gatsby 'opening a chest of rubies to ease, with their crimson-lighted depths, the gnawings of his broken heart'. This suggests that he wants to believe in Gatsby, in spite of his better judgement. The imagery he uses of flaming tigers and crimson-hearted rubies invokes the romantic idea of a flamboyant buccaneer who turned to piracy when his heart was broken, giving important insights into Nick's feelings about Gatsby and into why he helps Gatsby to seduce another man's wife.

When Gatsby offers Nick 'a little business on the side' (p. 80), it is obvious that the 'business' Gatsby offers is shady, if not downright illegal. However, Nick admits that the only reason he turned it down was because of the 'tactless' way in which it was offered. Gatsby clearly wishes to reward Nick, whom he is using to further his affair, but Nick seems to like to think that he is doing a friend a favour. Nick describes Gatsby as smiling 'like an ecstatic patron of recurrent light' (p. 86), suggesting that, overwhelmed by the ecstasy he imagines Gatsby is experiencing, he sees only the romance and not the betrayal.

Because Nick is appalled by Gatsby's sentimentality (p. 107), he rewrites Gatsby's account of his life. Whenever Gatsby's actual words are quoted, they are quite unimaginative, so it seems that the sentimentality, of which Nick disapproves, is not in the words but in Gatsby's unrealistic optimism that he can repeat the past: 'I'm going to fix everything just the way it was before.' By contrast, Nick is a romantic who finds beauty in the sense of loss. As he listens to Gatsby's account, he is reminded of something that he had heard somewhere a long time ago (p. 107). It seems to be something from his childhood, a time

> **TASK**
> Analyse Nick's reaction to the telephone call on page 110. Why does he lie about the butler's response?

when he was innocent, before he was corrupted or divided by desire. This elusive fragment is 'uncommunicable for ever' because he has changed and can no longer feel it. According to Nick, the younger Gatsby knew that once he kissed Daisy, he would abandon his aspirations to achieve something 'great', 'his mind would never romp again like the mind of God'. Perhaps Nick, too, once dreamed of being immortalised.

The day Gatsby died

modal auxiliary:
an auxiliary verb used to express the mood of the verb — often expressing a possible, rather than definite, action.
Can/could, will/ would, shall/should, may/might and must are all modal auxiliaries.

On pages 153–4, Nick writes an imaginary account of the events which led up to Gatsby's death. Fitzgerald uses the modal auxiliary 'must have' to indicate that this is Nick's interpretation, and that Nick only imagines Gatsby's feelings on the day he died. Nick thinks that Gatsby has lived for so long with his dream that his realisation of Daisy's desertion must transform his view of the world completely so that even a 'rose' is 'grotesque'. However, Nick sees only what he wants to see, and he distorts the facts to fit his imaginary interpretation.

If he was unable to get through to Gatsby on the phone, then Daisy may also have tried unsuccessfully to get through. If Gatsby had not yet received the important phone call, perhaps that is the message he is waiting for. If, as Nick assumes, Gatsby was expecting Daisy to call, and she was the most important thing in his life, why should he block the line at lunch time? Fitzgerald has created mystery around his eponymous hero by using an unreliable narrator, thereby ensuring that his novel continues to be the subject of intense debate.

Structure

The events of the story cover some 18 years, from when Gatsby wrote his schedule in September 1906, before leaving home and meeting Dan Cody in 1907, to when Nick supposedly finished writing his book in 1924. However, instead of a long-drawn-out story, Fitzgerald concentrates on just four months, fracturing Nick's narrative with accounts of past events told by different characters.

CRITICAL VIEW

In his book, *The Fictional Technique of F. Scott Fitzgerald* (1964), the critic, James E. Miller, Jr., plots the sequence of events in *The Great Gatsby* in this way:
'Allowing X to stand for the straight chronological account of the summer of 1922, and A, B, C, D, and E to represent the significant events of Gatsby's past, the nine chapters of *The Great Gatsby* may be charted: X, X, X, XCX, X, XBXCX, X, XCXDXD, XEXAX.'

For the most part, we are given information in the order in which Nick gets it, just as we might learn about a new acquaintance in real life, but at times he withholds information until later and sometimes he reveals things before he would have learned them. Our interest is aroused in Gatsby through hints and rumours before we meet him, and we learn nothing about his past until we have met the man himself. Even then his past is an enigma as Gatsby gives Nick contradictory information. We learn more about Nick's feelings about Gatsby than we do about the man himself, because he never tells his own story; Nick interprets for him.

Nick tells us on the second page that he is writing a 'book' whose title includes Gatsby's name. Towards the end of Chapter III, he pauses to read through what he has written so far and correct false impressions, quickly passing over the other events of his life in order to concentrate on the main story. In Chapter VI, he defends a narrative choice to deviate from his plan of unfolding events as he experienced them and to give us some of Gatsby's account of his early life 'with the idea of exploding those first wild rumours about his **antecedents**'. In Chapter VIII, he again presents something out of sequence and explains why. The final chapter is Nick's own story of the aftermath of Gatsby's death. Fitzgerald has made it appear that Nick has shaped his narrative, carefully deciding what to include and what to omit.

Scenic method

The material included in this novel is highly selective. Fitzgerald uses the scenic method of narrative construction which he admired in the novels of Henry James and Edith Wharton. He does not devote much time to telling us about what happens between these scenes; however, he does impart a lot of information very concisely. For instance, he deftly uses the list of names Nick writes on the timetable in Chapter IV to hint that Gatsby's story is only one of many narratives which could be developed further. He succinctly sets Gatsby's tragedy against a background of violent behaviour, sudden deaths, drunkenness, automobile accidents, murder, gambling, corruption on the stock exchange, divorce and suicide.

We know only what Nick finds out, and we have to piece the story together from the details he supposedly remembers, being aware all the time that Nick's interpretation is not necessarily the one Fitzgerald wants us to adopt. The scenes which Nick can describe first hand are either ones where he hears one person's account of events or social gatherings at which Nick is present.

Although the scenes are separate and self-contained, Fitzgerald does more than link them as different scenes in the story. He creates intricate patterns of imagery and symbolism, and some of the scenes parallel or contrast with others. For instance:

- In Chapter I, Daisy and Tom hold a dinner party for Jordan and Nick; the 'fifth guest' is the telephone, bringing Tom's 'other woman' as an intruder.
- In Chapter VII, Daisy and Tom hold a luncheon party; this time the fifth guest is Gatsby.
- In Chapters III, IV and VI, '**the world and its mistress**' flock to Gatsby's parties.
- In Chapter IX, Gatsby's funeral is attended by the postman, four or five servants, his father and only two of the guests who had come to his parties.

antecedents: a person's ancestors or extended family. Gatsby is rumoured to be Kaiser Wilhelm's cousin (p.35), nephew to Von Hindenburg and second cousin to the devil (p.60).

Taking it further ▶

In the film(s) you have watched, what scenes have been added? For instance, in the 1974 film we see Jordan cheating at golf and Wilson shooting Gatsby. How true do you think they are to the book?

TASK

Create a table to show the different types of social gatherings in each chapter.

Top ten quotation

TASK

Find parallels and contrasts between the scenes.

TASK

Draw a flowchart to trace how Fitzgerald uses the seasons as a structuring device in the novel and uses the weather to reflect or enhance the mood.

TASK

Choose a passage which you think demonstrates Fitzgerald's skills as a poet and set it out as a poem; then justify your choice. For an example, see **Extended commentaries** on page 96.

TASK

List the twelve violent deaths reported in the novel and make another list of the instances of violence against women.

- In Chapter V, Daisy and Gatsby sit side by side on a couch, so 'possessed by intense life' that they have forgotten about Nick, the observer.
- In Chapter VII, Daisy and Tom sit opposite each other while Nick, the peeping Tom, peers through the 'rift at the sill' where the blind does not totally obscure the window.

The weather contributes to the sense of passing time, and provides an appropriate mood for each scene. Fitzgerald uses the weather as a linking device between scenes.

Stylistic variety

Before starting to write *The Great Gatsby*, Fitzgerald re-read Joseph Conrad's advice to any novelist who aspired to produce a work of art. Conrad maintained that a great novelist:

cannot be faithful to any one of the temporary formulas of his craft. The enduring part of them, the truth which each only imperfectly veils – should abide with him as the most precious of his possessions, but they all: Realism, Romanticism, Naturalism, even the unofficial sentimentalism ... all these gods must after a short period of fellowship, abandon him – even on the very threshold of the temple – to the stammerings of his conscience and to the outspoken consciousness of the difficulties of his work.

(Preface to The Nigger of the Narcissus)

In *The Great Gatsby*, Fitzgerald has drawn on different generic styles and blended them together. Perhaps the most significant is one which Conrad did not mention. In the Foreword to his 1967 biography, Andrew Turnbull writes that 'Though an artist in prose fiction – with facets of the dramatist, the essayist and the social historian – Fitzgerald was fundamentally a poet.'

Poet

A poet is a creative artist of great imaginative and expressive capabilities and special sensitivity to language.

Social historian

Although Fitzgerald can write with lyrical romanticism, he never lets us forget the brutality and decadence of the society about which he writes. There is always an undercurrent of violence.

Essayist

Moralising

At times, Fitzgerald gives Nick a moralistic tone, and he makes pronouncements which he seems to think are self-evident truisms, such as: 'There is no confusion like the confusion of a simple mind' (p. 119) and 'Dishonesty in a woman is a thing you never blame deeply' (pp. 58–9).

Satirising

At other times it seems to be Fitzgerald himself who is the essayist, exposing faults or foolishness by inviting readers to laugh at them. In some places, Fitzgerald promotes his own values by mocking the values of the society he describes. An example of this is on page 53: 'The hall was at present occupied by two deplorably sober men and their highly indignant wives.' It is a common satirical device to pretend to accept the opposite of what you believe as the norm. Not only does Fitzgerald ridicule the party-goers for thinking it deplorable that anyone should be sober, but the sentence structure suggests that the wives are indignant because the husbands are sober.

Build critical skills

Explore the satire in this quotation from page 43: Gatsby's uninvited guests 'conducted themselves according to the rules of behaviour associated with an amusement park. Sometimes they came and went without having met Gatsby at all, came for the party with a simplicity of heart that was its own ticket of admission.'

Juxtaposing

Fitzgerald has deliberately placed ideas next to each other to achieve a particular effect. Daisy and Tom 'drifted here and there unrestfully wherever people played polo and were rich together'. The juxtaposition of playing a game and being rich is an ironic comment on the shallowness of the rich, who do nothing useful either with their money or to earn it. 'Drifting' and 'unrestfully' highlight the restlessness of the post-war generation and the aimlessness of their attempts to find things to do with their lives.

Build critical skills

Explain how Fitzgerald has used the following **oxymorons** to achieve a particular effect:

- 'harsh defiant wistfulness' (p. 13)
- 'winking ferociously' (p. 18)
- 'ferocious delicacy' (p. 69)
- 'ineffable gaudiness' (p. 95).

Fitzgerald also uses **paradoxes**, two of which are explored in the **Top ten quotations** section (numbers 9 and 10) – see pages 103–4.

Build critical skills

Analyse this quotation from page 41: 'men and girls came and went like moths among the whisperings and the champagne and the stars'. Explore what Fitzgerald achieves by juxtaposing 'whisperings' and 'champagne' with 'stars'.

oxymoron: two contradictory terms placed side by side which form a compressed paradox.

paradox: a self-contradictory truth, e.g. 'old friends whom I scarcely knew at all'.

nasal velar plosive: a consonant made by stopping the air flow completely and then releasing the air quickly with a small explosive sound and allowing the soft palate or 'vellum' to be lowered so that the air passes out through the nose as well as the mouth.

TASK

Make notes on the distinctive speaking style of each of the main characters.

Dramatist

Fitzgerald gives his narrator a distinctive and varied manner of speech that includes literary language and sophisticated vocabulary as well as more straightforward and direct turns of phrase. For example: 'In spite of the wives' agreement that such malevolence was beyond credibility, the dispute ended in a short struggle and both wives were lifted, kicking, into the night' (p. 53). The polysyllabic abstract nouns 'malevolence' and 'credibility' are followed by the abrupt dynamic verbs 'lifted, kicking'. This invites the reader to laugh at the women whose voluble complaints are defeated by brute force.

As well as using language to create a more fully-rounded narrator, Fitzgerald creates scenes using dialogue in which each character has a distinctive manner of speaking. Wolfshiem, for example, has a distinctive east European accent, using the nasal velar plosive /g/ instead of /k/ in 'business gonnegtion' and 'Oggsford College'. Like Myrtle, he uses 'of' instead of 'have', and non-standard grammar, such as 'It was six of us' (p. 68), 'He hadn't eat anything for a couple of days' and 'I knew I could use him good' (p. 162). Sometimes he speaks like a gangster with a controlling directness: 'I said "All right, Katspaugh, don't pay him a penny till he shuts his mouth." He shut it then and there' (p. 68). Sometimes he uses the first person plural imperative form like a clergyman: 'Let us learn to show our friendship for a man when he is alive and not after he is dead' (p. 163).

Symbolism

In literature, a symbol combines an image with a concept. Whenever we read a literary text, we bring our previous experience with us, so a writer knows that images will evoke particular associations in our minds. Fitzgerald expects us to have ideas about what the images he employs represent. When the same or similar images are used frequently throughout the novel, they achieve a particular resonance and increase in power.

The green light

Green represents new life, youth and hope, but also inexperience and naïvety. Green stands for grass, growth, and the natural landscape of newly-discovered territory. Travellers are given the green light as a signal that they can move forward. We bring these associations to our response to the green light, but it gradually achieves a special significance.

On page 25, Fitzgerald suggests that the green light is like a religious icon to Gatsby as he stretches out his arms towards it. Nick learns that Gatsby bought his house so that Daisy would be just across the bay, so to Gatsby the green light might offer encouragement, but the reader may feel that green suggests the naïvety of his dream that he can recreate the past, that Daisy will declare that she never loved Tom. On page 90, Gatsby mentions the light to Daisy, and Nick notes that 'he seemed absorbed in what he had just said. Possibly it had occurred to him that the colossal significance of that light had vanished for ever.' Nick suggests that the inaccessibility of his dream was what turned the green light into 'an enchanted object'. '**The green light**' which had seemed to symbolise an invitation to Gatsby to go ahead and to suggest the hope of a new life with Daisy, lured Gatsby to his death.

> Top ten quotation

Images of vision and insight

Nick is our eyes; we see only what he notices and comments on. This is explored in detail under **Themes: Reality behind appearances** on pages 29–30. He is aware of the importance of both the advertisement for Dr T.J. Eckleburg and the owl-eyed man.

Dr T.J. Eckleburg

The most haunting of Fitzgerald's many references to eyes are those which stare out from a huge billboard placed next to the railway line in the valley of ashes to attract travellers' attention. Each time Fitzgerald's characters went to town, 'the giant eyes of Doctor T.J. Eckleburg kept their vigil' (p. 118). Wilson takes Myrtle to the window to see the eyes and says 'God knows what you've been doing … You may fool me, but you can't fool God.' He assumes the eyes see everything, but these eyes are blind. Perhaps Fitzgerald, who was brought up as a Catholic but left the Church in 1917, is saying that there is no God watching over us; however, this symbol invites different interpretations.

The eyes are 'dimmed a little by many paintless days', just as people's spirituality has been dimmed by neglect. The 'wild wag of an oculist' placed the advertisement to 'fatten his practice' in one of the affluent areas of New York, but he has moved on. This uncaring materialistic society abandons the poor when it becomes clear that there is no money to be made. Society suffers from 'eternal blindness' or from forgetfulness. The advertisement is a reminder that people's vision needs correcting so they can appreciate the things that matter. Perhaps we are meant to think of God as a 'wild wag' who watches us making fools of ourselves and losing that clarity of vision needed to live by moral precepts. Fitzgerald's God, like the oculist, is merely absent, or mocking us for our failures.

On the other hand, Nick personifies the eyes as 'brooding' over the solemn dumping ground, suggesting that the presence they represent is disappointed by people's behaviour. Perhaps Fitzgerald is using the eyes to suggest a presence, whom some call God, that is watching over society all the time and will hold us accountable for our actions, even if we fool the people around us. Dreams of

Personification: referring to an object or animal as if it were human.

owning material possessions have replaced spiritual values. While the people who live in the valley of ashes are losing their dreams and dying, turning into ash or dust, Eckleburg, like Keats' Grecian Urn, will ironically live on and survive to represent the age of materialism.

'Owl-Eyes'

In the mythology of ancient Greece, Athena, goddess of wisdom, was so impressed by the great eyes and solemn appearance of the owl that she honoured the bird by making him her favourite. It was believed that a magical 'inner light' gave owls night vision. As the symbol of Athena, the owl was a protector, accompanying Greek armies to war, and it also kept a watchful eye on Athenian trade and commerce from the reverse side of their coins. By using this cruel childish nickname for one of Gatsby's guests, Fitzgerald suggests that this man also has vision and insight.

> **Top ten quotation**

'Owl-Eyes' sees past Gatsby's assumed persona and realises that, although the books are real, Gatsby has not read any of them. He mutters that 'if one brick was removed the whole library was liable to collapse', a hyperbolic statement which recognises that Gatsby's dream is founded **'on a fairy's wing'** (p. 96). However, he is not interested in the content of the books nor in Gatsby's reason for creating the illusion, he is content to be impressed by Gatsby's skills at stage-management. He has blinkered vision.

After the accident in Chapter III, Owl-Eyes, for all his apparent wisdom, cannot explain himself clearly and people are not receptive to the truth. They are, of course, drunk on alcohol illegally imported. Perhaps this is an ironic comment on the failings of a society which has given itself up to the 'pursuit of happiness' through such parties.

Owl-Eyes is the only one of Gatsby's party guests (apart from Nick) to attend his funeral. The rain obscures his vision, and he has to remove his glasses to wipe them. However, he is the only one to say 'Amen' to the murmur 'Blessed are the dead that the rain fall on', and he calls on his God to witness his shock that none of Gatsby's other visitors have come to the funeral.

Cars

For many Americans in the twentieth century, the car became a symbol of the American Dream. A car not only proclaims your social status, but it gives you freedom and independence. However, a car also symbolises the hopelessness of the poor, like Wilson, who can only dream of owning a car and going West.

Cars are associated with particular characters in different ways:

Context

In 1925 in the USA, cars were responsible for the deaths of 25,000 people, of whom 17,500 were pedestrians.

Gatsby

▲ How does this image of Gatsby's car compare with the one Nick describes?

For the young Gatsby, Daisy's house became a centre of romance, mystery and wealth, 'redolent of this year's motor cars' (p. 141). For him, cars are a symbol of wealth and power. He has a Rolls-Royce, a station wagon and an amazing car which Tom refers to as 'a circus wagon'. Nick describes it impressionistically on page 63, but this description fits no real car of the 1920s. It is appropriate that Gatsby, the man who reinvented himself at the age of 17, the man who builds his life on a dream, the man who turns his house into an imitation of the World's Fair, should have a car born of the fantastic dreams of a teenager. He shows it off to Nick with typical understatement: 'It's pretty, isn't it, old sport?'

NB see **Extended commentaries** on pages 97–8 for an analysis of the description of Gatsby's car.

The car, however, is not merely a symbol of his wealth; it is an outlet for his restlessness. Nick tells us that 'he was never quite still'. He takes Nick on a reckless detour: 'with fenders spread like wings we scattered light through half Astoria' (p. 66), until they attract the attention of the police.

Daisy

In her youth, Daisy had a 'little white roadster' which gave her the freedom to lead an independent life. As a married woman, she has a chauffeur who appears critical

Build critical skills

What other evidence can you find of Gatsby's restlessness? Why do you think Fitzgerald stresses this facet of his character?

of her visiting Nick at West Egg, suggesting that she may be under supervision. Daisy's attempt to have a glamorous affair, losing her nerve at the confrontation, is symbolised by her disastrous attempt to drive Gatsby's car at speed.

Tom

Tom usually travels to New York by train, so that Myrtle can join him without arousing suspicion. But his car gives him an excuse to go to her husband's garage, and he keeps Wilson sweet by repeatedly promising to sell it to him. Wilson refers to it as an 'old car', so clearly Tom does not regard it as a status symbol. Tom is a careless driver and, just after his return from his honeymoon, he 'ran into a wagon on the Ventura road one night and ripped a front wheel off his car' (p. 75). He races Gatsby (p. 119), and he is excited by the prospect of the crash (p. 131), before he realises that Myrtle is dead. A car gives Tom the freedom to have affairs, but it is something he finds useful rather than something he values.

Wilson

Cars are Wilson's livelihood, but he does not own a car and has to walk when he sets out to avenge Myrtle's death. The car in his garage is covered in dust, suggesting he has not worked on it for a long time. However, when Wilson finds out that Myrtle is having an affair, the car Tom has promised him offers the only hope he has of earning enough to leave the valley of ashes.

Jordan Baker

Jordan's name is composed of two American makes of car, reflecting her modern image.

TASK

List the five references to accidents involving cars which build up to the climax of Myrtle's death.

She drives recklessly, carelessly flicking a button on a workman's coat as she drives too close (p. 59). Her attitude is that other people should keep out of her way. The car represents her independence, but also the careless attitude of the rich. A curious conversation about driving between Nick and Jordan is actually about morality (p. 59). She later accuses Nick of being another bad driver (p. 168), explaining that she was wrong in thinking him to be an honest, straightforward person.

Cars represent mobility and independence; however, in this novel, they become a powerful symbol of the carelessness of the rich, as well as the hopelessness of the poor who can only dream of owning a car and going West. They are used as symbols of wealth and power, but they also represent the restlessness of the post-war generation.

Symbolic settings

New York (Manhattan)

New York is the financial centre where Nick works in bonds, the centre of the entertainment industry, particularly film production in Astoria, and also a place where the police are corrupt, and gangsters and gamblers disguise their operations behind apparently respectable office doors.

From a distance, the city rises like a fairytale landscape with 'its first wild promise of all the mystery and the beauty in the world'. However, those who paid for the buildings had gained their fortunes immorally. The reality beneath the façade of mystery and beauty is revealed to be small rooms, tastelessly furnished with pretentious furniture, people callously conducting extra-marital affairs, men who violently abuse women, and the defenceless and vulnerable (like the puppy) suffering at the whims of careless people.

For Nick, New York has a 'racy, adventurous feel ... at night'; however, he is an observer, 'wasting the most poignant moments of night and life'. Through the windows of the many taxis (five deep), he can see people being hurried 'towards gaiety' in the theatre district. This presents a significant contrast between those living the 'racy' life and the 'haunting loneliness' of the outsiders (pp. 57–8).

The valley of ashes

NB see the **Commentary to Chapter II** on pages 9–10 and **Extended commentaries** on page 97 for a detailed analysis of the symbolism of the valley of ashes.

East and West Egg

NB see the **Commentaries to Chapter I** on pages 5–8 and also **Chapter VI** on pages 15–16 for some detailed analysis of the difference between these two settings.

Nick explains why he thinks Daisy 'was appalled by West Egg; this unprecedented "place" that Broadway had begotten upon a Long Island fishing village – appalled by its raw vigour that chafed under the old euphemisms and by the too obtrusive fate that herded its inhabitants along a short-cut from nothing to nothing' (p. 103). When Fitzgerald was writing, Broadway had been famous as the centre of entertainment for over a hundred years, so it had the same connotations then as it does now. Fitzgerald explains that most of the residents of West Egg worked in the entertainment industry by using an image of birth, suggesting that Broadway fertilised the egg and a community was born that was characterised by 'raw vigour' and that 'chafed under the old euphemisms' used by the inhabitants of East Egg.

In East Egg, people seem constantly aware that there should be more to life, but they are unable to find it. People have aimless conversations like the one Jordan and Daisy have in the Buchanans' East Egg mansion: '"We ought to plan something" ... "All right... What'll we plan? ... What do people plan?"' (p. 17). Although both communities lead meaningless, empty lives, those at East Egg pretend to something more; they represent old money and pretend to represent old-established values. They buy their houses and expect to stay (p. 15), but they are unhappy, restless, searching for something else. Those at West Egg rent their houses for the season (p. 11) and enjoy themselves casually without any hang-ups: 'The air is alive with chatter and laughter, and casual innuendo, and introductions forgotten on the spot, and enthusiastic meetings between women who never knew each other's names' (p. 42).

Whatever their differences, both communities are going from 'nothing to nothing'. That is why Gatsby is so exceptional; at least he has a dream, even if it is unachievable. At least he believes in the green light. In 'the great barnyard of Long Island Sound' (p. 10), neither of the eggs is fertile; East Egg offers indifference and West Egg offers escapism, but neither community offers a future.

Patterns of imagery

In this novel, Fitzgerald is concerned to show how Gatsby managed to cherish a dream, keeping alive an idealised vision of Daisy, in a society where money and possessions define a person's value rather than their moral worth or their capacity for love. Fitzgerald uses imagery to convey the freshness and innocence of Nick's romantic appreciation of New York and of Gatsby's dream, and then contrasting imagery to convey the disillusionment as events unfold.

The future

Fitzgerald's use of imagery reveals a change in Nick's feelings about the future as the months pass. A day or so after his arrival in West Egg, he declares: 'And so with the sunshine and the great bursts of leaves growing on trees, just as things grow fast in the movies, I had that familiar conviction that life was beginning over again with the summer' (pp. 9–10). Here Fitzgerald offers a conventional romantic image of rebirth with trees bursting into leaf in the spring sunshine. However, he blends the natural image with a reference to the cinematic technique which speeds up the process. In this way, Fitzgerald manages to suggest Nick's enjoyment of the pace of life in the city, and that the future seemed exciting for a young man from the more rural Midwest.

Within only two or three months, on his 30th birthday, after Tom has confronted Gatsby in the Plaza Hotel, Nick observes, 'I was thirty. Before me stretched the portentous, menacing road of a new decade' (p. 129). Fitzgerald reveals his disillusionment through his image of the future as a road which Nick personifies as 'menacing'.

Windows

Through numerous references to windows, in each of which the observer's vision may have been distorted, Fitzgerald seems to be warning his readers to mistrust the perceptions of his narrator. This increases the mystery and ambiguity surrounding events.

NB see also **Themes: Reality behind appearances** on pages 29–30.

Women in white

Fitzgerald gives three images of women in white dresses at different points in the story:

- **Page 13:** 'an enormous couch on which two young women were buoyed up as though upon an anchored balloon. They were both in white, and their dresses were rippling and fluttering as if they had just been blown back in after a short flight around the house.'

  Nick has recently arrived in New York and is rather naïve. He describes Daisy and Jordan romantically as if they were fairies (or even angels) having just flown around the house. Before Daisy married Tom, her surname was Fay, a word which means fairy, and Nick seems enchanted by her ethereal quality. The white dresses suggest that their 'white girlhood' has not left them, and they are still pure and unsullied.

- **Page 110:** 'Daisy and Jordan lay upon an enormous couch, like silver idols weighing down their own white dresses against the singing breezes of the fans.'

  The next time he sees Daisy and Jordan together, two or three months later, in a similar position, their dresses are still white, but Nick's disillusionment is revealed to the reader through Fitzgerald's subtle change of colour. The two young women no longer seem like spirits of the air, now they are 'like silver idols', materialistic and spiritually inert, weighing down their own dresses.

- **Page 167:** 'In the foreground four solemn men in dress suits are walking along the sidewalk with a stretcher on which lies a drunken woman in a white evening dress.'

  After Gatsby is killed and Nick returns to the Midwest, his cynicism is revealed in the nightmares he has about West Egg. This time the woman in white is drunk; her hand which dangles over the side of the stretcher sparkles cold with jewels. 'No one knows the woman's name and no one cares.' Now, there is not even an illusion of warmth, life or friendship.

Breasts and nurturing; birth and eggs

Fitzgerald also reveals changes in Nick's perception through references to breasts and nurturing, birth and eggs.

Eggs

When he first arrives in 'the great wet barnyard of Long Island Sound' in the spring (p. 10), Nick projects his own sense of wonder onto the gulls. His life is 'beginning all over again' and Fitzgerald's choice to change the landscape to resemble eggs suggests that it is an appropriate place for him to hatch out into a 'well-rounded man'.

Birth

When Nick learns that Gatsby bought the house so that he would be near Daisy, he thinks he understands everything (p. 76). An image of birth suggests this revelation, writing of Gatsby's 'purposeless splendour' as a 'womb' from which he has emerged now that Nick knows why he has such an ostentatious lifestyle. It is Gatsby's dream that makes him come alive for Nick.

By August, Nick has lost his sense of wonder and excitement at the new life opening up to him. He thinks Daisy was 'appalled by West Egg, this unprecedented "place" that Broadway had begotten upon a Long Island fishing village' (p. 103).

Nurture

On page 107, Nick imagines the turning point in Gatsby's life to be when he kissed Daisy. Before that moment, in the moonlight, Gatsby felt that, alone, he could climb to a place where there was no limit to his aspirations, where life would feed his desires with the 'incomparable milk of wonder'. He knew that, once he kissed Daisy, she would become the incarnation of his dream, and, because she is human, with 'perishable breath', 'his mind would never romp again like the mind of God'. For this reason he hesitated before he lost this vision forever and transferred his aspirations to Daisy. In this image, it is life that has the potential to nurture Gatsby's imagination, and the milk suggests that he could return to a state of innocence.

Breasts

On page 110, Nick's cynicism is revealed in his description of Daisy. He notices little details like the 'tiny gust of powder' that rose from Daisy's 'bosom into the air' when she laughed. Although she is a mother, her 'bosom' is not used for nurturing but is cosmetically enhanced as part of the image she creates to attract men.

After the climactic scene in the Plaza Hotel, Nick has no illusions left. What he sees on the way back to East Egg is a brutal image of death. Myrtle's clothes are torn open to reveal 'her left breast swinging loose like a flap' (p. 131). Myrtle's breast is not a symbol of motherhood but of her sexuality. The image he evokes blatantly carries the message that the sexuality with which she betrayed her husband has brought about her death.

On the final page of the novel, Nick experiences for himself something of the vision that 'pandered in whispers to the last and greatest of all human dreams'. Once again moonlight creates an illusion, and he can imagine what it must have

Top ten quotation

been like to be one of the original settlers, seeing **'a fresh green breast'** of Long Island with its two eggs, for the first time. It is America that promises 'the incomparable milk of wonder', and the American Dream is revived for Nick in spite of his close encounter with the reality. The final words of the novel reveal that Nick, like other Americans, will continue to '**beat on, boats against the current, borne back ceaselessly into the past**'.

Top ten quotation

Precious metals and jewellery

Fitzgerald also reveals Nick's attitudes in references to precious metals and jewellery. On page 64, Gatsby tells Nick that, when he 'lived like a young rajah', he collected 'jewels, chiefly rubies'. When he then shows Nick the photograph from Oxford, Nick's imagination transforms Gatsby into a romantic buccaneer, 'opening a chest of rubies'. The jewels are plunder, but in Nick's fantasy they have 'crimson-lighted depths' and console the 'gnawings' of his hero's 'broken heart'. On page 90, when he observes that Gatsby quickly changes the subject to avoid talking about Cody's yacht, Nick says that he 'was going to ask to see the rubies when the phone rang'.

The epigraph on page 5, which suggests that the woman is moved because her lover wears a gold hat, is presumably supposed to have been added by Nick after the events of the story, when he started writing the book. This fragment was actually written by Fitzgerald, and it warns us in advance that Nick (or is it Fitzgerald?) intends us to see Daisy as shallow, attracted to Gatsby by his wealth and his showmanship. If she has no deep feelings for him, it is inevitable that she will let him down. His efforts to 'move her' are doomed to disappointment.

Nick's fairytale description of Daisy as 'High in a white palace the king's daughter, the golden girl' (p. 115) places her as an object of desire, out of reach because of her wealth; Nick is a romantic, but he is also aware of reality, and he interprets Daisy's charm as her inaccessibility. When Nick interprets how the young Lieutenant Gatsby had felt about Daisy, he uses a **simile** saying she is 'gleaming like silver, safe and proud above the hot struggles of the poor' (p. 142). This romantic description is once again tainted with the belief that Daisy's attraction lies in her wealth, especially since it comes immediately after he says that Gatsby 'took Daisy one still October night'. Nick's imagery reveals his attitude that Daisy is an object, 'silver', and the double meaning of 'safe' suggests that she is both protected by her wealth and inaccessible because of it.

Nick's cynicism about Daisy is also revealed in the fact that he specifies the amount of money Tom spent on Daisy's string of pearls, suggesting that he thinks that Daisy is mercenary, even though it is Jordan who has given him this information. Then, at the end, Nick sees Tom go into the jewellery store and speculates, in a deceptively casual tone, that he might be going 'to buy a pearl necklace – or perhaps only a pair of cuff buttons'. Daisy already has a string of pearls, so these suggestions reveal that he assumes Tom has another woman, and is immoral, like Wolfshiem. As he states, he is rid of his 'provincial squeamishness for ever'.

Build critical skills

For AO5, you must explore different interpretations. Do you think Fitzgerald wants us to think that Nick is being romantic or cynical when he says this?

simile: a comparison introduced by 'as' or 'like'.

The heat and the sweat

Fitzgerald chose to set the climax of his story on the hottest day of the year. The imagery Nick uses links the increasing tension to the heat. On page 109, Fitzgerald uses synaesthesia, blending the senses of hearing and feeling to enhance the stifling atmosphere. The National Biscuit Company 'whistles' are 'hot', and the 'hush' is described as 'simmering', a metaphor which compares the heat with a liquid, simmering on the stove, possibly in danger of boiling over and scalding someone. The tension increases as they set off for Manhattan, and the heat is more intense. The gravel is like a 'blazing' fire, no longer threatening merely to scald, but to burn. By the time they reach the garage and the tension has increased because Wilson has found out that Myrtle is having an affair, Nick personifies the heat as 'relentless', having no compassion, and 'beating', making him feel physical pain (p. 118).

Once in the room at the Plaza, Nick is no longer an onlooker; he is involved and feeling 'the heat and the sweat' in a very uncomfortable way. He is sweating profusely and his underwear 'kept climbing like a damp snake' around his legs. A snake has biblical connotations of betrayal, suggesting a subconscious guilt on Nick's part for his role in bringing Daisy and Gatsby together again. As Daisy rises to Gatsby's defence, the tension is so strong that 'The compressed heat exploded into sound'. It feels as if the hot air is compressed and stifling them, and, when the orchestra strikes up below, Fitzgerald once again employs synaesthesia to blend the senses of hearing and feeling so that it seems as if the tension explodes. This is the crisis point. Mendelssohn's 'Wedding March' evokes shared memories of Tom and Daisy's wedding, from which Gatsby is excluded, and these give Tom the advantage so that Daisy no longer defends Gatsby by threatening to leave when Tom starts to goad Gatsby about Oxford.

Target your thinking

- In what ways is your reading of the novel enriched by your understanding of its contexts? Refer to specific parts of the text as you respond. (**AO3**)
- Which other post-war writers explore themes similar to those developed by Fitzgerald? (**AO4**)
- In what ways can knowledge of other critics' comments about *The Great Gatsby* help us to form our own opinions? (**AO5**)

Biographical context

Francis Scott Fitzgerald emerged onto the literary stage when new technology was creating celebrities, and those who courted publicity often became victims of the media's insatiable appetite for 'news'. Fitzgerald's reputation gives an unfair impression of him, and, to really appreciate *The Great Gatsby*, it is important to separate the man from his public persona. Nevertheless, his early rise to stardom, his reckless celebrity lifestyle, his romantic but troubled marriage, his decline into alcoholism and his premature death have come to represent the spectacular boom and bust years of his era: the Roaring Twenties and the Depression.

Throughout his life, Fitzgerald was split between his need to write and his desire to experience life so that he could write about it. He embraced new experiences with energy and enthusiasm, but always with that degree of detachment which enables a writer to collect material. He wrote, by his own admission, 'blindly, incessantly'.

It was Fitzgerald's infectious love of life which led him to books and to writing. He was impetuous, energetic, a tease who liked to be teased. The biographer Andrew Turnbull wrote that 'Fitzgerald ... saw the beauty of life and wanted to celebrate it and make others see it. There was something soaring and idealistic in his nature which constantly reached out for the experiences he hadn't had.'

Fitzgerald had that sense of the infinite, of life's mystery, which we associate with writers of the Romantic period like his favourite poet, John Keats. Like the Romantic poets, his perception of a writer was someone who lives life intensely so that he can write about his own feelings with a heightened perception. While he was looking for intensity of experience to give depth to his writing, America entered the Great War.

Fitzgerald desperately wanted to go to the war and enlisted in May 1917. However, he was unable to commit himself to anything other than writing,

Build critical skills

Gatsby has fallen in love with a rich girl who rejected him, and overheard someone remark that 'poor boys shouldn't think of marrying rich girls'. How far do you think these experiences sowed the seeds for *The Great Gatsby*?

Build critical skills

Where in the novel does Fitzgerald celebrate the 'beauty of life'?

and he put his literary ambitions above military training. He was caught in the dilemma of whether to experience life or to write about it. When the war ended, Fitzgerald still had not been thought ready to be sent overseas. At training camp, he met Zelda Sayre, a kindred spirit with a similarly uninhibited and reckless love of life, with whom he fell passionately in love. She was from a socially prominent family and refused to marry Fitzgerald until he was a financial success. When he was discharged, he went to New York to make his fortune as a writer. Like Nick Carraway, at first Fitzgerald found in New York the 'wild promise of all the mystery in the world'.

Fitzgerald was a divided soul. He wanted to write, but, while he was writing, he worried that he was missing out on living. He wanted to be a serious writer, but he also wanted to make a great deal of money. When Zelda broke off their engagement, he was freed from the need to make money quickly, so he returned to his parents while he edited and improved his novel. In 1920 it seemed he could have it all. In February he had a short story published; his novel, *This Side of Paradise*, was published in March and was well received; and he married Zelda in April.

Context

'The uncertainties of 1919 were over - there seemed little doubt about what would happen - America was going on the greatest, gaudiest spree in history and there was going to be plenty to tell about it. The whole golden boom was in the air - its splendid generosities, its outrageous corruptions, and the tortuous death struggle of the old America in prohibition.'

(F. Scott Fitzgerald, *My Lost City: The Crack-Up*, 1962)

Build critical skills

How far would you say that *The Great Gatsby* illustrates 'the tortuous death struggle of the old America'?

Writing *The Great Gatsby*

The Great Gatsby is seen as *the* novel of the Roaring Twenties because Fitzgerald depicts both the 'golden boom' with its 'splendid generosities' and the 'tortuous death struggle of the old America'.

Fitzgerald was living the American Dream; he was young and good-looking, and he had earned money and early success through his own hard work. However, already he and Zelda were partying wildly, drinking excessively and making exhibitions of themselves, just to get into the news. Fitzgerald himself acknowledged that he 'was pushed into the position not only of spokesman for the time but of the typical product of that same moment' (*My Lost City: The Crack-Up*, 1962).

Fitzgerald adored Zelda, but they had a very stormy relationship. She did not understand his ambition to be the best novelist of his generation; he was always afraid that he might lose her. In September 1922, the couple rented a house near Great Neck, Long Island, and they embarked on a riotous year which provided the background for *The Great Gatsby*.

◀ F. Scott Fitzgerald and Zelda

The residents of Manhasset Neck were descendants of families who had made their fortunes in the nineteenth century. Across the bay, Great Neck was a popular residence for newly-rich theatrical people who held extravagant parties. However, it would be a mistake to think that Fitzgerald was as careless and thoughtless as his characters. Although he was generous and wasteful with the money he earned, his Midwestern puritanism deplored his improvidence, and he atoned for it with intensive periods of work. Even though he hated having to write stories for magazines, he was a perfectionist and would shut himself away to earn enough money to allow him to concentrate on his serious novel.

Over the next two years, he wrote three short stories in which he prepared the ground for *The Great Gatsby*. 'Winter Dreams' and 'The Sensible Thing' are both about the loss of dreams, and 'Absolution' was originally intended as an early chapter of his novel, telling the story of Gatsby's childhood.

In many ways, *The Great Gatsby* is a product of Fitzgerald's attempts to confront his own conflicting feelings about the Jazz Age. He was seduced by the wild and extravagant life of the rich, and he wanted to be at the heart of it, like Gatsby, but he was also aware of the moral emptiness and the hypocrisy beneath the excitement.

Historical context

America before the Great War

European settlers first arrived, in the sixteenth and seventeenth centuries, hoping to leave behind the old country with its prejudices and hierarchy and forge a new life where hard work was the key to success. However, what brought the Dutch traders to Long Island was a desire for profit. The Dutch West India Company intended to exploit the natural resources of the New World, symbolised in Nick's vision by the destruction of the trees that had made way for Gatsby's house.

Context

In his short story 'The Swimmers', written in 1929, Fitzgerald wrote about 'a sense of overwhelming gratitude and gladness that America was there, that, under the ugly débris of industry, the rich land still pushed up, incorrigibly lavish and fertile, and that in the heart of the leaderless people the old generosities and devotions fought on, breaking out sometimes in fanaticism and excess, but indomitable and undefeated.'

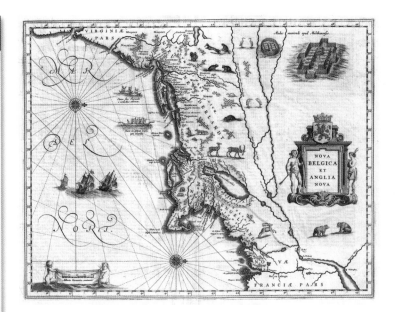

▲ 1635 map of New York

The American Dream

This concept has its roots in the American Declaration of Independence in 1776. The Founding Fathers set out their vision in the justification for breaking away from British rule: 'We hold these Truths to be self-evident that all men are created equal, that they are endowed, by their Creator, with certain unalienable Rights, that among these are Life, Liberty and the Pursuit of Happiness.' (See **Themes: The American Dream** on pages 23–4 and **Literary context: Early American writers** from page 72.)

America often portrays itself as a 'melting pot' to describe the process of immigration and colonisation by which different nationalities, cultures and races were to blend into a new utopian community. It presents itself as a land of freedom and opportunity for all, although, originally, 'all' meant only Northern European men, as Fitzgerald makes clear.

Context

These words are inscribed on the pedestal of the Statue of Liberty - the New World addresses the old:

'Give me your tired, your poor,

Your huddled masses yearning to breathe free

The wretched refuse of your teeming shore.

Send these, the homeless, tempest-tossed to me,

I lift my lamp beside the golden door!'

(Emma Lazarus, 1849-87)

Industrialisation

The Industrial Revolution offered another way to make a fortune, but, instead of bringing progress and increased order, the safety and welfare of the workers were often neglected in the pursuit of profit. Industrialisation turned the United States into a great world power, and made a few people wealthy, but it also created 'the valley of ashes'.

Social context

Post-war America

The outbreak of the war took most Americans by surprise. They were horrified but also relieved that they were not involved. Even when the *Lusitania* was sunk in May 1915, killing 128 Americans, President Woodrow Wilson only sent a formal letter of protest to Germany. In January 1917, Germany resumed unrestricted submarine warfare, sinking American ships, so, reluctantly, America joined the war in April.

By September 1918, more than a million American troops were involved, and, in the Battle of Argonne, at which both Nick and Gatsby were supposedly present, they inflicted one of the great defeats on the Germans which helped to bring an end to the war. Those who survived the war thought of it as having been a pointless and destructive slaughter in which they had been forced to participate because of the ineptitude of their parents' generation.

> **Context**
>
> 'Americans had entered the fight under the assurance that it was a crusade - or at any rate in the expectation of fun and heroics in the Old World at the government's expense. They left the scene sure that they had been duped: that it was not, after all, their war.'
>
> (Marcus Cunliffe, *The Literature of the United States*, 1954)

> **Context**
>
> Nearly 120,000 Americans died in the Great War and more than 200,000 were wounded.

> **Build critical skills**
>
> How successfully do you think Fitzgerald illustrates the disillusionment and restlessness of those who returned from the war?

The Roaring Twenties

Peace meant that munitions, uniforms, food and other provisions for the army were no longer in demand. Inflation continued to be extremely high and loans to the Allies ceased in 1920, so Europeans could no longer buy American exports. President Harding's administration was plagued by scandal and corruption, and his efforts to rebuild the American economy were opposed both by unions and by organised crime, the leaders of which wielded immense power. President Harding and his successor, Calvin Coolidge, supported management in labour disputes in the hope of rebuilding the wealth of the country. They brought in tax legislation which benefited the wealthy, widening the gap between rich and poor.

> **Build critical skills**
>
> How does Fitzgerald make his readers aware of the widening gap between rich and poor in the novel?

TASK

On page 16, Tom 'took down his drink as if it were a drop in the bottom of a glass'. How many other references to alcohol consumption can you find?

Nevertheless, for the country, the 1920s was a period of uninterrupted economic progress. This was the decade that changed the image of America from a log cabin to a thrusting skyscraper. New York City's role as an ever-growing world trade centre, together with the rising prices of building plots, encouraged many ambitious companies to commission skyscrapers.

Prohibition

Depression in agriculture led to migration from farms to cities, changing the face of America. In 1920 more Americans were living in towns than in the country. However, rural America, the home of white Protestants who still held to Benjamin Franklin's virtues of thrift, hard work and self-denial, achieved a dramatic victory which helped shape the next decade: on 16 January 1920, the Eighteenth Amendment to the Constitution outlawed the manufacture, transportation and sale of intoxicating liquor.

The demand for alcohol was increased by Prohibition, and ruthless bootleggers, like Al Capone, made millions of dollars through illegal alcohol sales. Gangsterism provided a means of rapid upward mobility for unscrupulous men.

The economy

Boom

The total of national wealth rose dramatically in the 1920s. This economic boom was fuelled by new industries, bringing recent inventions such as automobiles, refrigerators and telephones to many American homes. These industries needed iron, steel, glass, rubber and, of course, roads, so these industries also boomed. The new products had to be advertised, so the advertising industry blossomed and huge billboards were placed beside highways and railways, like that for Dr T.J. Eckleburg.

The boom was directly experienced by only a privileged minority; however, the mass-production of radios and the proliferation of magazines and newspapers meant that ordinary people could enjoy this life from the sidelines. It was not only the movie industry which filled the gossip pages. People became passionate about spectator sports and sporting celebrities. The boom in the leisure industry made it possible for women like Jordan to become sports celebrities.

For the first time, ordinary people could realise their dreams; however, most could not afford to buy goods outright, having to use hire purchase agreements. Many people were trapped in debt and could only dream that one day they would make the breakthrough. As mass-production revolutionised the automobile industry, the car became a potent symbol of the age. It provided mobility to almost everyone, and it gave a new social freedom to young women.

Bust

In spite of the economic boom, there were more than 600 bank failures every year. Businesses put their profits into investments, and employees were encouraged to spend their savings on buying stock in the company, and even to buy 'on the margin', buying with money they did not have, intending to pay their creditor out of the profits when the shares were sold. There were no effective means for ensuring that bankers or stockbrokers were honest. The financiers of New York were the same type of people who had formerly exploited the Wild West, and they brought the same capacity for selfish exploitation to the bond market.

Eventually, the bubble burst, and the Wall Street Crash of 1929 brought an end to the Roaring Twenties. Fitzgerald was writing *The Great Gatsby* five years before the stock market crash, and, although he could not have foreseen this particular event, there is a strong suggestion that, unless the hedonistic lifestyle of the young people whom Tom and Daisy represented was curbed, it would lead to disaster: 'they smashed up things and creatures and then retreated into their money or their vast carelessness … and let other people clean up the mess they had made' (p. 170).

Racial issues

Fitzgerald also reflects the contemporary attitude of white supremacy — the belief that white people are superior to other races, and the fear of immigrants who were not white Anglo-Saxon Protestants. Tom is reading *The Rising Tide of Color*, written by Lothrop Stoddard in 1920, a book which gave authenticity to this belief through claims of scientific racism. Business leaders lobbied against immigrants who they believed were taking jobs away from American citizens. In response, Congress passed a series of laws setting immigrant quotas and discriminating against people from Southern and Eastern Europe and from Asia.

NB see **Ethnic criticism** on page 77.

Cultural context

New York City

Fitzgerald puts New York at the centre of American business, wealth, the entertainment industry, crime and social exclusiveness, using a wealth of detail which locates the novel precisely in the early 1920s. However, he does not take a documentary approach. Even the geography of the area is changed to fit his purposes, and the allusions are made with a lightness of touch which creates an impressionistic picture as the backdrop to a story of urban America.

Geography

Fitzgerald sets his novel just outside the city boundary as well as on Manhattan Island. He has not only made up new names for what were, actually, Great Neck and Manhasset Neck, but he also changed the shape, creating 'a pair

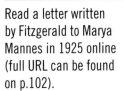

Taking it further ▶

Read a letter written by Fitzgerald to Marya Mannes in 1925 online (full URL can be found on p.102).

Consider what light this analysis of his feelings about America throws on our understanding of *The Great Gatsby*.

Context

After the war, race riots broke out in the North, where former slaves from the South had gone to fill the war-built factories, and in the South a new Ku Klux Klan began to arise, viciously attacking Jews and Catholics as well as African Americans.

of enormous eggs'. The tip of Manhasset was an enclave of the fashionable, respectable wealthy, whereas Great Neck was home to those who had acquired their fortunes more recently, and more adventurously. When they travel to the city, Fitzgerald's characters have to cross 'a small foul river', in the valley of ashes.

Context

The Astoria Studio was the centre of the American film industry, until Hollywood lured the industry to a location where the weather was more predictable and land not so expensive.

Context

Flushing Creek used to meander through salt marshes until it reached Flushing Bay on the East River, but, in the nineteenth century, the growing borough of Brooklyn acquired the land and gave it to the Brooklyn Ash Removal Company. This company turned the salt marshes into a landfill site for garbage, horse manure and ashes from coal-burning furnaces.

When Jay Gatsby drives to the city, he passes the fictional Port Roosevelt and takes Nick on a detour through Astoria, presumably to show off his car.

Taking it further ▶▶

Find a street map of Manhattan Island and find these locations:

1. Nick dines at the Yale Club on Grand Central Terminus between 44th and 45th Streets.

2. He strolls down Madison Avenue [west of and parallel to Park Avenue], past the old Murray Hill Hotel, and over 33rd Street to the Pennsylvania Station.

3. The residents of Long Island drive over Queensboro Bridge to reach Manhattan

4. They pass over Blackwell's Island [now known as Roosevelt Island].

5. Nick had lunch with Gatsby and Wolfshiem in a well-fanned cellar in 42nd Street.

6. Wolfshiem prefers the old Metropole Hotel 'across the street', where Rosy Rosenthal was shot in 43rd Street.

7. Jordan and Nick talk in the tea-garden at the Plaza Hotel, on the south side of Central Park. This is also where Gatsby, Daisy, Tom, Nick and Jordan engage the parlour of a suite on the hottest day of the summer.

8. Jordan and Nick drive through Central Park in a Victoria, a fashionable horse-drawn carriage for two passengers.

9. They walk down 59th Street, towards Queensboro Bridge.

10. Jordan suggests that 'Those big movies around Fiftieth Street are cool'.

11. After Gatsby's death, Nick visits Wolfshiem at his office on Broadway.

12. Wolfshiem tells Nick that he met Gatsby in Winebrenner's pool-room on 43rd Street.

The entertainment industry

▲ A still of one of Gatsby's parties from Baz Luhrmann's 2013 film

There are various references to people in the entertainment industry as Nick describes Gatsby's parties. Among the real people mentioned are Joe Frisco, a vaudeville performer, and Gilda Gray, a popular dancer who appeared in the Ziegfeld Follies on Broadway. The owl-eyed man compares Gatsby with David Belasco, who was famous for bringing a new standard of naturalism to the American stage, creating sets which paid great attention to detail, and thus Fitzgerald confirms that Gatsby's house is a set to support the part he is playing.

Organised crime

Prohibition was an extremely difficult law to enforce, and people could acquire as much alcohol as they wanted. In rural areas, people made their own hooch (or moonshine) with illegal stills, but, in towns, people relied on bootleggers to satisfy their demands. Those with money, like Tom, could easily get hold of alcohol and felt justified in doing so, which effectively blurred the lines of demarcation between what was legal and illegal, moral and immoral. By 1925, there were about 100,000 illegal drinking dens, or speakeasies, in New York City alone, and Fitzgerald indicates that much of Gatsby's fortune comes from selling alcohol illegally.

Arnold Rothstein

Fitzgerald's source for Meyer Wolfshiem was Arnold Rothstein, a New York businessman and gangster who became a famous kingpin of organised crime and was widely reputed to have been behind baseball's Black Sox Scandal in which the 1919 World Series was fixed. Fitzgerald emphasises Wolfshiem's

CRITICAL VIEW

'the further the 1920s recede, the more the novel emerges as one of the most penetrating criticisms of that incredible decade' (Dan Piper, *The Great Gatsby: The Novel, The Critics, The Background*, New York: Scribners, 1970)

Jewish race, suggesting that, since the establishment was the preserve of the 'Nordics', whom Tom Buchanan calls the 'dominant race', for other cultural groups, gambling and crime seemed to be the only way to build up a fortune.

Fitzgerald draws attention to the corruption of the police when Wolfshiem reminisces about 'Rosy' Rosenthal and also when Gatsby explains that he 'was able to do the commissioner a favour once and he sends me a Christmas card every year'.

Literary context

Romanticism

Instead of prizing reason and logical thinking, the Romantics insisted that the emotional side of human responses was more important, that the brain should learn from the heart and from natural instinct, that the imagination held purer truths than the mind.

Fitzgerald wrote the following when he was advising his daughter to read some poetry:

> *'Poetry is either something that lives like fire inside you … or else it is nothing … **The Grecian Urn** is unbearably beautiful … About the tenth [reading] I began to know what it was about, and caught the chime in it and the exquisite inner mechanics. Likewise with **The Nightingale** which I can never read without tears in my eyes.'*
>
> *(Letter to Scottie Fitzgerald at Princeton University, August 1940)*

In 'Ode to a Nightingale', Keats dramatises the desire to lose oneself completely in a moment of exquisite happiness. Writing the poem at some point after the experience, he manages to evoke his spontaneous feelings at the time when he was listening to the nightingale. In *The Great Gatsby*, Fitzgerald emulates Keats' ability to write about a memory with all the freshness and spontaneity of the moment he experienced it. Unlike Keats, however, for whom nature was all-important, Fitzgerald found Romantic images indoors. Instead of merely aping nineteenth-century writers, Fitzgerald took Romanticism and reconstructed it to fit 1920s urban America.

NB see **Themes: Urban Romanticism** on page 28.

Early American writers

The original Romantics rejected urban life for nature, but the rural landscape in Europe was very different from the dramatic wild landscapes of America with their extreme climate, and the Native Americans, fighting desperately to protect their way of life. A new genre of novels emerged based on the life of cowboys and pioneers in 'The Wild West'. Novels like *Hopalong Cassidy* (1904), on the flyleaf of which James Gatz had written his schedule, had rude and rough-talking heroes, but fed people's dreams with stories of legendary possibilities for new opportunities and individual freedoms.

Fitzgerald modelled Gatsby's schedule on that of Benjamin Franklin, who had written under a pseudonym in *Poor Richard's Almanac*, an annual publication which included memorable sayings such as: 'Early to bed and early to rise, makes a man healthy, wealthy and wise'. These aphorisms optimistically sold dreams of wealth made by leading a simple lifestyle.

Reverend Horatio Alger also wrote stories in which, through hard work, determination, courage, and concern for others, his characters achieved wealth and success. These books all fostered among Americans a belief that the American Dream was within their reach, if they worked hard enough. However, like young Gatz, many did not follow Alger's advice on how to achieve it, regarding wealth as essential for the pursuit of happiness, which the Declaration of Independence had declared was an 'unalienable right'. Significantly, Wolfshiem suggests that Gatsby achieved wealth through honest effort and industry when he says 'I raised him up out of nothing, right out of the gutter.' Fitzgerald challenges the moral naïvety of Alger's books in *The Great Gatsby*, because none of his characters has achieved success solely through hard work.

> aphorism: opinion phrased like an obvious truth, e.g. 'There is no confusion like the confusion of a simple mind' (p. 119).

Realism

However, towards the end of the nineteenth century, there were writers who felt it their duty to portray American life realistically. Mark Twain rejected Romanticism to write about people and society as he saw them, and in so doing exposed the hypocrisy of a Christian society which practises slavery. In offering an unbiased, accurate representation of society, and confronting the problems of the individual, Realists expose the hypocrisy of 'civilised' society.

Fitzgerald adds realistic touches to his Romantic descriptions which neatly puncture the hypocrisy of society. Gatsby bought a factual imitation of some Hôtel de Ville in Normandy, built in the twentieth century. The owner's children had been in such a hurry to sell the house that they did not leave time to grieve; it still had the black wreath on the door. As a final realistic detail, Nick saw a maid appear at an upper window and spit into the garden.

Even Nick's romantic evocation of the arrival of the Dutch sailors is tinged with realism as he describes how the trees 'pandered' to them. The verb 'pander' has derogatory connotations from Shakespeare's Pandarus who is presented as a cynical pimp. Fitzgerald's implication here is that the freshness of the New World, symbolised by the trees, encouraged the sailors to plunder the land. He suggests a corruption at the heart of the American Dream which occurred when European settlers made nature into a commodity.

Henry James developed the scenic method that Fitzgerald employs in *The Great Gatsby*, constructing a narrative by linking a series of scenes that Nick Carraway witnesses. James' novella *The Turn of the Screw* (1898), may have given Fitzgerald the idea of using an unreliable narrator to create ambiguity.

Naturalism

In rejecting Romanticism as well as the belief that man can shape his own future, Realists laid the foundation for Naturalism, in which characters were portrayed as victims of social forces over which they had little or no control. Naturalists usually explored working-class characters, through their relationships with their urban surroundings. One of the most influential writers was Upton Sinclair, who exposed corruption in the Chicago meat-packing industry by focusing on the appalling living and working conditions of the poor, the exploitation of women and children in the factories and the hopelessness prevalent among the workers.

Fitzgerald's portrayal of the valley of ashes and the despair of the 'ash-grey men, who move dimly and already crumbling through the powdery air', provides a stark contrast with the lives of the wealthy and exposes their lack of social conscience. Even Nick, who seems to empathise with their hopelessness, hypocritically fails to tell the truth at the inquest and so leaves the tragic Wilson branded as a madman.

Modernism

Fitzgerald revived Romanticism by blending its imagery with the modern world. Throughout the novel, Fitzgerald uses words we associate with Romanticism, such as 'bloomed', 'singing breeze' and 'enchanted', and juxtaposes them with words and images from the modern world. At the Buchanans' mansion, 'the crimson room bloomed with light' from electric bulbs; 'the singing breeze' describes the hum of electric fans. The 'enchanted' green light which represents Gatsby's hopes and dreams is an electric light, installed to guide boats (possibly smuggling alcohol) on Long Island Sound.

Fitzgerald was one of the key post-war writers to employ realistic and naturalistic techniques to spearhead a Modernist movement. Modernism was an international movement which advocated innovation in all the arts. In America especially, a literature was needed that would explain what had happened and what was happening to their society. Modernist writers were concerned to reveal the way people think. It is the internal world, rather than the external world which is important, and Fitzgerald uses complex patterns to explore this.

In *The Great Gatsby*, what really counts is not the novel's plot, but the effect of events on Nick, the narrator. To explore Nick's thoughts and feelings fully, the others remain shadowy because we are given no insight to their inner thoughts and feelings. Without this, we either rely on Nick's interpretation, or we draw assumptions from his observations of their expressions or behaviour.

For Modernists the specific was more important than the general, so, in *The Great Gatsby*, we always know exactly where we are, both geographically and chronologically. Fitzgerald evokes specific pieces of music and describes detailed fashions. His minor characters are linked by specific references to the worlds of organised crime, entertainment, business or finance. Yet the novel is by no means a documentary. Fitzgerald uses real details as artists working on collage might use cuttings from magazines and newspapers to evoke a specific era as they explore their themes.

By employing a narrator who is a relatively minor participant in the story but from whose point of view the reader learns about events, Fitzgerald, like Henry James and Joseph Conrad, gives his readers a series of scenes with the most significant parts either left to the imagination or reported through a third party. Joseph Conrad developed this narrative technique in *Lord Jim* (1900) and in *Heart of Darkness* (1902), and, like Conrad, Fitzgerald holds back key events and reveals them in a different order to enhance the mystery around Gatsby and to produce an intricately complex narrative structure.

Symbolism

Modernist writers were influenced by Freud's theory of an image-language of dreams; they attacked society's problems by using symbolism to make their own judgements on American life. Fitzgerald's symbol of the eyes of Dr T.J. Eckleburg, for instance, is a powerful indictment of contemporary American life.

NB see **Writer's methods: Symbolism** on page 53 for a discussion on Dr T.J. Eckleburg.

Another powerful image is Dan Cody's yacht, which, Nick tells us, represented for the young James Gatz, 'all the beauty and glamour in the world'. Thus Fitzgerald links Gatz's romantic dreams with the sordid materialism of Cody's past as a 'pioneer debauchee' who had made his fortune in a climate of 'savage violence'.

The Great War had a deep impact on American thought and development. Like other post-war works, *The Great Gatsby* conveys a mood of disillusionment with society and despair at its loss of values. It is a story of a careless, aimless, materialistic society of vast wealth which tramples over the sterile world of the poor. He makes a direct reference to Upton Sinclair's *Main Street* (1920) to help to evoke the mood of the valley of ashes, and he also quotes the title of T.S. Eliot's poem 'The Waste Land' (1922), which offers similarly bleak images of sterility, death and despair in the post-war world. Fitzgerald echoes the emptiness of the woman's life in Eliot's poem who asks 'What shall we do tomorrow? What shall we ever do?' when Daisy asks: 'What'll we do with ourselves this afternoon? … and the day after that, and the next thirty years?'

NB see also **Commentary to Chapter II** on pages 9–10.

'A work ... of art'

Before beginning *The Great Gatsby*, Fitzgerald re-read Joseph Conrad's preface to *The Nigger of the Narcissus* (1897), and this had a significant influence on his writing of the novel. Conrad felt very strongly that the novel was an art form, and, 'A work that aspires, however humbly, to the condition of art should carry its justification in every line.' Fitzgerald followed this advice closely and so it is important to realise that he has chosen every word carefully.

Build critical skills

In Chapter VIII, Fitzgerald withholds the information that Wilson called at the Buchanans' mansion before going to Gatsby's house. Why do you think he did this?

Taking it further

Read Conrad's Preface to *The Nigger of the Narcissus*, and assess its impact on Fitzgerald: www.online-literature.com/conrad/the-narcissus/0

Critical context

Contemporary criticism

When *The Great Gatsby* was published in 1925, many reviewers recognised it as a fulfilment of the promise Fitzgerald had shown in his previous novels. Isabel Paterson wrote in 1925 that, 'Mr Fitzgerald managed somehow to pour his glowing youth on the page before it could escape forever.' She praised the novel for being more carefully crafted than his first. However, she did argue that Fitzgerald's chief weakness was his superficiality.

Others, such as H.L. Mencken, were more overtly critical. He called the novel a 'glorified anecdote', complaining that it is 'simply a story', and that 'only Gatsby himself genuinely lives and breathes'. He dismissed the other characters as 'mere marionettes'. Nevertheless, he was full of praise for Fitzgerald's craftsmanship and 'The obvious phrase is simply not in it. The sentences roll along smoothly, sparklingly, variously. There is evidence in every line of hard and intelligent effort.'

Gertrude Stein told Fitzgerald in a letter that he was 'creating the contemporary world' in the same way that W.M. Thackeray had in his novels. This is a significant choice of verb, implying that he was not merely reflecting 1920s America but helping to construct it. T.S. Eliot was also 'interested and excited' by the novel, grandly claiming that it represented 'the first step that American fiction has taken since Henry James'.

Posthumous revival

In spite of its largely favourable reception by the critics, the novel did not sell well. However, when Fitzgerald died in 1940, at the age of 44, his death re-awakened interest in his books. Several obituaries praised *The Great Gatsby*, but some felt that it was already outdated. Fitzgerald's writing was linked to his life, and his decline into alcoholism was seen by some as related to his supposed inability to fulfil his early promise.

William Troy

Nevertheless, several new editions appeared in the 1940s, and William Troy claimed that it was a characteristically American novel. He argued that Fitzgerald manages to achieve something like T.S. Eliot's 'objective correlative' by splitting his own divided self between the two central characters.

He is able to observe objectively through 'the ordinary but quite sensible narrator', as well as to bring to life, in Jay Gatsby, Fitzgerald's own romantic dreams. Troy claimed that Gatsby was a 'mythological creation', a product of the wish-fulfilment of a whole nation: 'Indeed … Gatsby becomes much more than a mere exorcising of whatever false elements of the American Dream Fitzgerald felt within himself: he becomes a symbol of America itself, dedicated to "the service of a vast, vulgar and meretricious beauty"' ('Scott Fitzgerald – The Authority of Failure', *Accent* magazine, 1945).

Build critical skills

What do you think Isabel Paterson meant when she said that Fitzgerald's characters are 'the froth of society, drifting sand along the shore'?

Build critical skills

How far do you agree that the minor characters are 'mere marionettes'?

objective correlative: an external equivalent for an internal state of mind.

Troy observed that the novelist had employed the technical device of an involved and sympathetic narrator, in the tradition of Henry James and Joseph Conrad, which makes for 'some of the most priceless values in fiction – economy, suspense, intensity. And these values *The Great Gatsby* possesses to a rare degree.' By linking Fitzgerald with established writers such as T.S. Eliot, Henry James and Joseph Conrad, Troy was signalling that *The Great Gatsby* was worthy of academic study.

Arthur Mizener

Another 1940s critic who rated the novel highly was Arthur Mizener. Like Troy, he explored the novel's 'modified first-person form' and Nick's importance as narrator. He called the novel a kind of 'tragic pastoral', with the East representing urban sophistication as well as corruption, and the West representing simple virtue. Mizener explored the title of the novel, observing that, 'In so far as Gatsby represents the simple virtue which Fitzgerald associates with the West, he is really a great man; in so far as he achieves the kind of notoriety which the East accords success of his kind, he is great about as Barnum was.' He judged that the irony of the book lay in Gatsby's inability to understand himself and how society judged him. Mizener recognised that, though a novelist, Fitzgerald was fundamentally a poet, and he praised the 'formal perfection' of *The Great Gatsby*.

The New Criticism of the 1950s

In the 1950s, *The Great Gatsby* achieved the status of a classic American novel. Lionel Trilling agreed with Troy that Gatsby represents America: 'Gatsby, divided between power and dream, comes inevitably to stand for America itself. Ours is the only nation that prides itself upon a dream and gives its name to one, "the American Dream".'

The academic debates had begun. In 1955, R.W. Stallman argued that it has become a great novel because Gatsby is a modern Icarus who 'belongs not exclusively to one epoch of American civilisation but rather to all history inasmuch as all history repeats in cycle form what Gatsby represents – America itself'.

Troy argued that Nick was an admirable character who had grown in moral perception by the end of the novel; Stallman disagreed, calling him 'a prig with holier-than-thou-airs'. Mizener had interpreted the novel as a 'tragic pastoral', celebrating an idealised version of rural life in the Midwest; whereas Stallman argued that Fitzgerald showed that the apparent division between the corrupt urban East and the moral rural Midwest exists only in Nick's imagination. Since these essays, many critics have joined in the debates and written books analysing *The Great Gatsby*.

Ethnic criticism

Fitzgerald's narrator, Nick Carraway, is expressing contemporary society's prejudices when he writes stereotypically about the 'three modish negroes,

CRITICAL VIEW

Do you agree with Troy that Gatsby comes to stand for America itself, or do you agree with Judith Fetterley – 'it is Daisy herself that is America, the fresh, green breast of the new world' – and think that Gatsby stands for American dreamers who exploit America in pursuit of their dreams?

CRITICAL VIEW

To what extent do you agree that, in *The Great Gatsby*, the West represents 'simple virtue'?

Context

Icarus is a character in Greek mythology who attempted to escape from exile using wings made from feathers and wax. He flew too close to the sun; the wax melted, and he fell into the sea. He is a common literary symbol of heroic audacity.

Context

In the USA in the first half of the twentieth century, Jews were discriminated against in employment, universities, membership of organisations and access to residential areas. Jews were one of the targets of the Ku Klux Klan.

two bucks and a girl', and then laughs 'aloud as the yolks of their eyeballs rolled towards [Gatsby's splendid car] in haughty rivalry' (p. 67). Similarly, when he mocks Meyer Wolfshiem, the 'small flat-nosed Jew' (p. 71), he is voicing society's anti-Semitism. It is more difficult to explain his mockery of his housekeeper, the 'demoniac Finn' (p. 84), and her heavy 'Finnish tread' (p. 82). Fitzgerald's use of a first person narrator means that the racist attitudes of his characters are not necessarily his, but, to a modern reader at least, they provide an ironic reflection on the American Dream and the words inscribed on the Statue of Liberty.

Not until 1947 was Fitzgerald first criticised for anti-Semitism. Not until 1967 was he criticised for his derogatory portrayals of African Americans, as well as the way Nick interprets the American Dream as being only for people like himself. In 1973, Peter Gregg Slater observed that Native Americans were ignored in Nick's vision of the founding moment of America. It is easy to criticise the novel for its narrow outlook, but it reflected the attitudes of the 1920s. We should be wary of judging Fitzgerald for being a product of his time.

Feminist criticism

In some male-centred references, such as when Nick says 'for a transitory enchanted moment man must have held his breath in the presence of this continent', Fitzgerald could be using generic terms, referring to both men and women; however, given Nick's misogynistic comments about women and behaviour towards them, it seems unlikely. When the novel failed to sell well, Fitzgerald himself suggested that this might be due to the aversion of female readers to the emotionally passive and undeveloped female characters. It was in the 1970s, however, that the rapid rise of feminism introduced new debates about the novel.

Feminist critics question the long-standing dominant male ideologies, patriarchal attitudes and male interpretations in literature. They challenge traditional and accepted male ideas about the nature of women and how women are, according to male writers, supposed to feel, act, and think. Fitzgerald limits his portrayal of his women characters by having as his narrator a misogynist who declares that 'Dishonesty in a woman is a thing you never blame deeply'. Such a narrator cannot be expected to reveal any empathy with a woman's feelings.

In 1977, Judith Fetterley published *The Resisting Reader: A Feminist Approach to American Fiction*, in which she argues that, at the time she was writing, American literature had been mostly written by men and so their attempts to define what it means to be American were made from a male perspective. She argues that, in *The Great Gatsby*, Fitzgerald portrays America as female, writing of her green breast which 'had once pandered in whispers to the last and greatest of all human dreams', whereas the dreamers are male. 'Daisy's failure of Gatsby is symbolic of the failure of America to live up to the expectations in the imagination of the men who "discovered" it. America is female; to be American is male; and the quintessential American experience is betrayal by a woman.'

Judith Fetterley also claims that *The Great Gatsby* is a classic male drama of poor boy achieving wealth and challenging rich boy, and that the story is a struggle for power with the prize being the girl. When the poor boy dies, it is not the rich boy who becomes the scapegoat, but Daisy, because in the end she failed him. Nick shakes hands with Tom, but there is no such reconciliation with Daisy; she alone bears the blame.

Homoerotic criticism

Lionel Trilling in 1951 was the first to suggest that Nick is attracted to Jordan Baker because she is like a boy, with her 'erect carriage, which she accentuated by throwing her body backward at the shoulders like a young cadet', but it was not until the more liberal attitudes of the 1970s that the issue began to be explored in more detail. In 1979, Keath Fraser wrote an essay in which he explores homoerotic undertones in the scene between Nick and Chester McKee. In 1924, Fitzgerald could not openly suggest a homosexual relationship, but the details and symbolism of the short scene strongly suggest it. He also explores Nick's fascination with Tom's powerful physique (p. 12). However, although Nick is seduced by Gatsby's 'rare' smile, he gives no description of his body, only his clothes. What he feels for Gatsby is not homoerotic but somehow protective; he is upset when the Sloanes are rude to him. He wants Gatsby to be happy.

Psychoanalytic Criticism

Psychoanalytic critics see literature as like dreams. Both are fictions, inventions of the mind that, although based on reality, are, by definition, not literally true. The theory is that much of what lies in the unconscious mind has been repressed by consciousness and emerges only in disguised forms, such as dreams, or in an art form, such as painting or writing. They interpret the author's purpose in writing as being to gratify secretly some forbidden wish which has been repressed into the unconscious mind.

Fitzgerald was writing *The Great Gatsby* at the time when psychoanalytic ideas and techniques were being developed and circulated. Freud first discussed his structural model of the psyche in his 1920 essay 'Beyond the Pleasure Principle', introducing his concepts of the 'id', the 'ego' and the 'super-ego'. These concepts were formalised and elaborated upon three years later in *The Ego and the Id*. According to Freud's theory, the id represents our inner desires, amoral and egocentric, ruled by the pleasure/pain principle. The super-ego is a symbolic internalisation of our upbringing and cultural regulations which acts as our conscience. The ego's task is to find a balance between these two opposing forces so that we can function in the real world.

Fitzgerald followed his inner desires and followed (or rather led) the decadent lifestyle of his generation, but his tragedy was that his super-ego made him despise himself for doing so. Like Fitzgerald himself, Nick Carraway shows evidence of being torn between his id and his super-ego, **'simultaneously enchanted and repelled by the inexhaustible variety of life'**.

CRITICAL VIEW

How far do you agree with Judith Fetterley that 'Not dead Gatsby but surviving Daisy is the object of the novel's hostility and its scapegoat'?

Context

Sigmund Freud (1856-1939) was a Jewish-Austrian psychiatrist who founded psychoanalysis. His originality made him one of the most influential thinkers of the early twentieth century.

Top ten quotation

Nick has a highly developed super-ego, therefore his upbringing leads him to disapprove of the other characters in the novel. However, his id, representing his inner desires, encourages him to forgive Gatsby, excusing his dishonesty because he admires, and perhaps envies, Gatsby's romantic vision. Thus he is able to present Gatsby as 'great', a tragic hero. He tells his readers at the beginning that he was both repelled and enchanted by Gatsby who 'represented everything for which I have an unaffected scorn', but 'there was something gorgeous about him, some heightened sensitivity to the promises of life'.

Nick's imagination and his dreams offer the key to understanding his character and how the events in the novel change him. On page 57, we learn that his ego tries to balance his desires and his conscience through a dream of secret casual affairs with romantic women to whom he does not have to commit himself. Fitzgerald uses a driving metaphor to explain how Nick's super-ego is preventing him from indulging his id, and from forming meaningful relationships: 'I am slow-thinking and full of interior rules that act as a brake on my desires.'

By the time he returns to the Midwest, Nick's 'fantastic dreams' are of West Egg, as if in 'a night scene by El Greco' (p. 167). No longer does he find the metropolitan twilight 'enchanting'; even the moon has lost its lustre and romance, and the sky appears 'sullen', an example of the pathetic fallacy which neatly sums up his disappointed romantic dreams.

Marxist criticism

The Marxist perspective is that works of literature are conditioned by the economic and political forces of their social context. Fitzgerald explores wealth and poverty in New York society, as well as class tensions between East Egg and West Egg. He gives valuable insights into the negative aspects of the post-war economic boom. His novel can be read as a penetrating criticism of the uncaring, materialistic and corrupt ruling classes.

Central to the story is the allegation that, at the inquest, the authorities put the blame for Gatsby's murder on Mr Wilson, 'in order that the case might remain in its simplest form'; to investigate the truth might have uncovered corruption at a high level. Both George and Myrtle Wilson are victims of the rich and powerful.

Ongoing debates

The richness and ambiguity of Fitzgerald's writing ensures that *The Great Gatsby* will continue to inspire debate about such topics as whether Gatsby can be called 'great', whether there is evidence that Daisy betrayed Gatsby, and whether Nick Carraway is a reliable narrator. Nick's deliberate vagueness about Gatsby's death has also turned the novel into a 'whodunnit', allowing discussion about whether Wilson really did kill Gatsby and then himself. Fitzgerald's rich use of imagery still gives critics opportunities to offer fresh insights into the meanings of the central symbols, such as the eyes of Dr T.J. Eckleburg and the green light at the end of Daisy's dock.

Context

Karl Marx (1818–83) was a German philosopher and political theorist. With Friedrich Engels, he was the author of *The Communist Manifesto* (1848), which interpreted society in terms of class struggle.

> **A05**   Explore literary texts informed by different interpretations

To fulfil the demands of this Assessment Objective, you can refer to the opinions of critics and/or you can explore different interpretations that you can offer from your own reading of the novel. Because Nick is an unreliable narrator, there are plenty of opportunities for you to explore different interpretations of events. You may think that his presentation of Daisy and Jordan is unsympathetic and judgemental, for instance, and offer another possible reading of the detailed observations he makes. Nick accepts the inquest's findings that Wilson murdered Gatsby. However there is evidence which suggests that Fitzgerald intended to raise the possibility that this might have been a contract killing, carried out by a hit man hired by one of Gatsby's business associates.

Building skills 1: Structuring your writing

This 'Building skills' section focuses on organising your written responses to convey your ideas as clearly and effectively as possible. More often than not, if your knowledge and understanding of *The Great Gatsby* is sound, a disappointing mark or grade will be down to one of two common mistakes: misreading the question or failing to organise your response economically and effectively. In an examination you'll be lucky if you can demonstrate 5 per cent of what you know about *The Great Gatsby*; luckily, if it's the right 5 per cent, that's all you need to gain full marks.

Understanding your examination

It's important to prepare for the specific type of response your examination body sets with regard to *The Great Gatsby*. You need to know if your paper is **open book** or **closed book**, as the format of your assessment has major implications for the way you organise your response and dictates the depth and detail required to achieve a top band mark.

Open book

In an open book exam, such as that set by AQA, when you have a copy of *The Great Gatsby* on the desk in front of you, there can be no possible excuse for failing to quote relevantly, accurately and frequently. To gain a high mark, you are expected to focus in detail on specific passages. Remember, too, that you must not refer to any supporting material such as the Introduction contained within the set edition of your text. If an examiner suspects that you have been lifting chunks of unacknowledged material from such a source, they will refer your paper to the examining body for possible plagiarism. You will gain no credit for quoting the explanatory notes at the back of your edition.

Closed book

In a closed book exam, such as that set by OCR, because the examiners are well aware that you do not have your text in front of you, their expectations will be different. While you are still expected to support your argument with relevant quotations, close textual references are also encouraged and rewarded. Again, since you will have had to memorise quotations, slight inaccuracies will not be severely punished. Rather than a forensically detailed analysis of a specific section of *The Great Gatsby*, the examiner will expect you to range more broadly across the novel to structure your response.

Step 1: Planning and beginning: locate the debate

A very common type of exam question invites you to open up a debate about the text by using various trigger words and phrases such as '**Consider the** view that …' or **'Discuss how far you agree with this view?'** When analysing this type of question, remember that exam questions never offer a view that makes no sense at all, nor one so blindingly obvious that all anyone can do is agree with it; there will always be a genuine interpretation at stake. They will expect you to offer evidence in agreement as well as evidence to refute the statement, and then come to a balanced conclusion, so logically your introduction needs to address the terms of this debate and sketch out the outlines of how you intend to move the argument forward to orientate the reader. Since it is obviously going to be helpful if you actually know this before you start writing, you really do need to plan before you begin to write.

Plan your answer by collecting together points for and against the given view. Aim to see a stated opinion as an interesting way of focusing upon a key facet of *The Great Gatsby*, like the following students.

Student A

This is the opening of an answer to the following AQA Specification A-style examination question:

Compare the ways in which the powerful feelings associated with love affect people in two of the texts you have studied. You should write about one prose text and at least two poems.

Fitzgerald presents love as being so powerful that it commits a person entirely to another, even if that person is inaccessible. According to Nick Carraway's interpretation of events, Gatsby 'committed himself to the following of a grail' when he first met Daisy and 'took what he could get, ravenously and unscrupulously'. It is not the predatory love-making that Fitzgerald equates with passion, but the pure love which makes Gatsby devote himself to Daisy, just as the most pure of Arthur's knights devoted themselves to the quest for the Holy Grail, the legendary cup in which Joseph of Arimathea is supposed to have caught the blood of Christ on the cross.

Similarly, the feelings that grip Thomas Wyatt's speaker in 'Who so List to Hount' are still strong, even though the woman he loves has been claimed by a more powerful man. Whereas Fitzgerald uses the spiritual association of the Grail to define Gatsby's quest, Wyatt uses a more physical extended metaphor of hunting a deer, which, at first sight, seems closer to the manner in which Gatsby 'took' Daisy before he went to war. However, Wyatt leaves the reader in no doubt that he has never caught her. His 'travail' has been in 'vain', and yet his passion appears undimmed, and he continues to follow her, though 'faynting'.

Examiner's commentary

This student:

- addresses the key words of the question ('compare', 'powerful feelings', 'love') in the first paragraph, setting up a strong line of argument to explore through the essay and demonstrating a perceptive understanding of both texts
- selects one significant point of connection to develop in detail, analysing relevant aspects of form and language in an assured manner
- pinpoints important quotations and integrates them into the syntax of the essay, confidently making connections between the texts
- comments meaningfully on AO2 by connecting the metaphorical language in each text
- expresses a confident personal view by exploring two possible ways of interpreting the poem.

If the rest of the essay reached this level of performance, and at least one other poem is covered, it is likely the student would be on course to achieve a notional grade A.

Step 2: Developing and linking: go with the flow

In the main body of your writing, you need to thread your developing argument through each paragraph consistently and logically, referring back to the terms established by the question itself, rephrasing and reframing as you go. Ensure your essay doesn't disintegrate into a series of disconnected building blocks by creating a neat and stable bridge between one paragraph and the next. Use discourse markers (linking words and phrases, like '**however**', '**although**' and '**moreover**') to connect the individual paragraphs of your essay and signpost the connections between different sections of your overarching argument.

Having set out an idea in Paragraph A, in Paragraph B you might need to then support it by providing a further example; if so, signal this to the reader with a phrase such as '**Moreover**, this imagery from hunting can also…' To change direction and challenge an idea begun in Paragraph A by acknowledging that it is open to interpretation, you could begin Paragraph B with something like '**On the other hand**, this view of Gatsby's passion could be challenged when …' Another typical link is when you want to show that the original idea doesn't give the full picture. Here you could modify your original point with something like '**Although** it is possible to see Nick's interpretation as a product of his Romantic imagination, the fact that Gatsby ignores all the women at his parties supports the idea that his passion for Daisy is single-minded.'

Student B

This sample is taken from the middle of an answer to the following AQA Specification A-style examination question:

Compare how the authors of one prose text and at least two poems you have studied present impediments to love.

Another impediment to Gatsby and Daisy's love presented in *The Great Gatsby* is the fact that Daisy has a mind of her own. Gatsby is certain that he can recreate the past, and he believes so strongly in his dream that he has convinced himself that Daisy never loved Tom and that she will leave him now that Gatsby is rich. However, Daisy cannot deny that she once loved Tom and that she is now a mother. Through Nick's description of the confrontation, Fitzgerald presents Daisy as a helpless victim. Even before Tom tells her of Gatsby's criminal activities, she cries to Gatsby: 'Oh, you want too much!' and, 'in a pitiful voice', refuses to say she never loved Tom. Nick may see her as 'pitiful', and sobbing 'helplessly', but a feminist critic would interpret his observations as showing that, in spite of the merciless way in which these two men are trying to control her, Daisy is a strong woman who knows her own mind, and, in spite of the emotional wrench, she refuses to tell a lie.

Similarly, the woman in Thomas Wyatt's poem, whom he thinks of metaphorically as a 'tame' deer, a man's natural prey, is 'wylde for to hold'. Like Daisy, she assumes a tame, helpless demeanour, but it is not only the fact that she belongs to 'Caesar' that is the problem for the lovers. Reluctantly, Wyatt admits that he seeks 'to hold the wynde', a metaphor which suggests that the woman is a free spirit and, with hindsight, this poem might have served as a warning to Henry VIII that Anne Boleyn was no tame possession.

Examiner's commentary

This student:

- ▼ confidently addresses the key words of the question: 'compare', 'how', 'present' and concentrates on the ways in which the two authors use aspects of language to create meaning
- ▼ uses well-chosen discourse markers, 'another' and 'similarly', to signpost the flow of ideas
- ▼ creates good cohesion between paragraphs by clearly connecting the stages of the argument

- ❑ integrates and develops quotations fluently
- ❑ perceptively explores different interpretations for AO5
- ❑ reveals a perceptive understanding of the historical context of Wyatt's poem but, instead of just adding it on, uses it to make a personal observation.

If the rest of the essay reached this level of performance and at least one other poem was covered, it is likely the student would be on course to achieve a notional grade A.

Step 3: Concluding: seal the deal

In your conclusion, you need to capture and clarify your response to the given view and make a relatively swift and elegant exit. Keep your final paragraph short and sweet; now is not the time to introduce any new points. However, don't just reword everything you have already just said either. Neat potential closers include:

- ❑ looping the last paragraph back to your introduction to suggest that you have now said all there is to say on the subject
- ❑ reflecting on your key points in order to reach a balanced overview
- ❑ ending with a punchy quotation that leaves the reader thinking
- ❑ discussing the contextual implications of the topic you have debated
- ❑ reversing expectations to end on an interesting alternative view
- ❑ stating why you think the main issue, theme or character under discussion is so central to the novel
- ❑ mentioning how different audiences over time might have responded to the topic.

Student C

This sample is taken from the conclusion of an answer to the following OCR-style examination question:

'Much American literature explores the issue of white supremacy in American society.'

By comparing *The Great Gatsby* with at least one other text prepared for this topic discuss how far you agree with this view.

Unlike Mark Twain, Fitzgerald does not seem to challenge the prejudices of New York society at the time. He has chosen as his narrator a man who has been brought up with a strong feeling of the superiority of people like himself. He laughs aloud at African Americans and mocks Wolfshiem for his Jewish

Extended commentaries

These three commentaries give close detailed analysis of key points in the novel. They are not intended to reflect examination essays.

The valley of ashes, pages 26–7

To describe the valley of ashes, Fitzgerald uses adjectives from the semantic field of disbelief, words which suggest an unnatural landscape beyond the range of human experience, such as 'grotesque', 'fantastic' and 'transcendent'. However, most of the adjectives come from a semantic field of sterility and despair: 'desolate', 'ash-grey', 'powdery', 'leaden', 'impenetrable', 'bleak', 'paintless', 'solemn', 'foul', 'dismal'.

The valley of ashes is the grim underside of New York, but an essential part of it. On one level, this 'waste land' represents the grey, dismal environment of the Wilsons and the class to which they belong, ignored and abandoned by the wealthy who pollute it. The valley is close to the lines of communication between the homes of the rich and the city, but there is no station at the valley of ashes. The trains pass straight through, although they are forced to stop when barges are moving in and out of the creek. Ironically, however, this 'dumping ground' is the inevitable end of the material possessions of the wealthy.

Fitzgerald draws a direct comparison between a fertile farm where crops are grown and this valley where 'ashes grow like wheat'. The whole landscape is created out of ash, and even the men who work there look as if they are formed out of ash. The farming metaphor emphasises by contrast the infertility of the valley, and it is significant that Myrtle and her husband have no children. Even the grey cars give out a 'ghastly' creak, as if they are giving up the ghost before coming to rest.

The only colour in the valley of ashes is provided by the blue and yellow oculist's advertisement that dominates it and three yellow brick shops. One of these is Wilson's garage. Fitzgerald's choice of yellow brick surrounded by grey makes it sound 'anaemic', like Wilson himself. Wilson is 'spiritless' and his garage is a 'shadow', insubstantial and lacking in life and vitality. 'Everything in the vicinity' is veiled in dust, including the only car in the building, a wrecked Ford. The garage seems to represent all those people whose lives have been destroyed by the affluent society, and who are now ignored and abandoned. Even Nick, with his romantic imagination, is unable to see in it any more than a grotesque parody of rural life elsewhere. He assumes that 'sumptuous and romantic apartments were concealed overhead', but he is wrong.

Gatsby's car, page 63

Gatsby has bought an enormous house across the Sound from Daisy, and he throws extravagant parties every weekend. Another way in which he hopes to attract Daisy's attention is by having a unique and extremely noticeable car. In two abrupt simple sentences, Nick observes: 'I'd seen it. Everybody had seen it.' To describe its enormous size, he compares it with a monster, which suggests disapproval in spite of his 'admiration', and calls it 'swollen' because of all the boxes which are piled on it and which Nick personifies as 'triumphant'.

To describe the windscreens, he extends the monstrous metaphor by evoking the Minotaur, as the car is 'terraced with a labyrinth of wind shields that mirrored a dozen suns'. His car takes natural light and multiplies it twelvefold, reinforcing the flamboyance of a wealthy man who wants to be noticed. However, Nick's use of 'monstrous' and 'swollen' reflect his snobbery. Gatsby represented everything for which Nick had 'an unaffected scorn', and this flashy need to be noticed suggested that deep down Gatsby was still the teenager from a poor family who rowed out to the luxury yacht that 'represented all the beauty and glamour in the world'.

Even allowing for Nick's enthusiastic hyperbole, this car sounds most unsafe to drive, since the glare from one sun can temporarily blind a driver. Nick draws a comparison with sitting in a conservatory, emphasising that they are detached from the outside world. In spite of the bright sunshine, Gatsby drives with all the lights on: 'With fenders spread like wings we scattered light through half Astoria.' It seems that Gatsby wants to fly up to Daisy, 'the golden girl', 'high in a white palace'. He seems to hope that the car will help him 'bounce high', like the gold-hatted lover in the epigraph.

Appropriately, Gatsby chose 'a rich cream colour' for his car, to reflect the image he wished to project of a golden, sunlit hero, in pursuit of a 'grail'. However, once the car has become what newspapers bluntly call 'the death car', the image changes, and witnesses describe it as 'yellow' and 'pale green', sickly rather than golden.

The car ultimately comes to symbolise the tragedy of the American Dream. Gatsby pursued happiness, as was his 'right' according to the Declaration of Independence, written by the Founding Fathers. When he achieved wealth, he commissioned a fabulous car which flamboyantly announced his arrival, but it was this symbol of his wealth and success that destroyed his dreams.

Nick concludes that the tragedy is that, like Gatsby, Americans reach out to the 'orgastic future' without realising that they have already lost it in their pursuit of it. It was Gatsby's efforts to achieve the American Dream and to create a beautiful and pure future for the woman he loved that enmeshed him in a lifestyle that brought about his destruction.

Gatsby's death, page 154

Andrew Turnbull wrote that 'Fitzgerald was fundamentally a poet'. One passage which could be restructured as a poem is the description of what Nick saw when he hurried down to the pool:

The swimming pool

There was a faint, barely perceptible movement of the water

As the fresh flow from one end urged its way toward the drain at the other.

With little ripples that were hardly the shadows of waves,

The laden mattress moved irregularly down the pool.

A small gust of wind that scarcely corrugated the surface

Was enough to disturb its accidental course with its accidental burden.

The touch of a cluster of leaves revolved it slowly,

Tracing, like the leg of a transit, a thin red circle in the water.

Unlike the brutally realistic description of Myrtle's body, Fitzgerald has not mentioned Gatsby's body at all. The readers are distanced from Gatsby in death as we were in life, so that nothing will destroy the illusion. There is no expression of shock or horror, and this suggests that Nick knew what they were going to find.

Reading this paragraph in isolation, there is no indication of its subject; instead, Nick seems mesmerised by the movement of the water. As the water starts to drain away, the mattress moves irregularly down the pool towards the drain, and, when most of the water has gone, the vortex carries the mattress round in gradual circles, and it seems to the fanciful Nick as if it were the touch of autumn leaves which provoked this circular motion.

Fitzgerald employs poetic techniques such as personification ('the water … urged its way'), alliteration ('fresh', 'flow from'), assonance ('touch … cluster') and rhythm (note, for instance, the regular iambic metre of the fourth line), to show that Nick finds a tragic romance in the death of a man whose life has not been heroic. Metaphors ('shadows', 'corrugated') give the detail, not to events, such as the opening of the drain, not to Gatsby's body, but to the surface of the water, showing that Nick is so mesmerised by its movement that he fails to notice what the people with him are doing. The repetition of the adjective 'accidental' turns Gatsby into a sacrificial victim because, in Nick's view, he was not the intended victim of the gunman. Fitzgerald's choice of adjective provides a neat play on words which creates ambiguity since 'accidental' can mean both unintentional and fateful.

Separating this passage encourages us to concentrate on Fitzgerald's skill as a poet, but it is important to look at it in the context of the book, as it continues patterns which Fitzgerald has woven through the whole novel. Fitzgerald has given it a cyclical movement: Nick came East in spring, the love affair blooms through the summer until the climax on the hottest day of the year, Gatsby dies on the first day of autumn when red leaves are already falling, and Nick returns to the Midwest in winter.

Throughout the novel, Fitzgerald has blended the natural and man-made worlds in his imagery. Here, too, the ripples on the water are so slight as to be hardly the 'shadows' of waves, but when a small gust of wind comes, the surface of the water looks like 'corrugated' paper or iron. A technological image compares the revolving mattress with the leg of a precision instrument, a transit compass, drawing a circle in the leaves. The movement of the mattress on the water is part of a recurring pattern of stillness and movement which started on page 13 when a breeze blew in through the windows of Daisy and Tom's house and 'rippled over the wine-coloured rug, making a shadow on it as the wind does on the sea'.

Top ten quotations

Before studying this section, you should identify your own 'top ten' quotations. Choose those phrases or sentences that seem to capture a key theme or aspect of the text most aptly and memorably, and clearly identify what it is about your choices that makes each one so significant. No two readers of *The Great Gatsby* will select exactly the same set, and it will be well worth comparing and defending your choices with the other students in your class.

When you have done this, look carefully at the following list of quotations and consider each one's possible significance within the novel. Discuss the ways in which each might be used in an essay response to support your exploration of various elements or readings of *The Great Gatsby*. Consider what these quotations tell us about F. Scott Fitzgerald's ideas, themes and methods, as well as how far they may contribute to various potential ways of interpreting the text.

'…what foul dust floated in the wake of his dreams…' (p.8)

1

⊣ Nick casts the blame for his disillusionment with people, not on Gatsby but on 'what preyed on Gatsby'. Gatsby's dreams are compared with a boat, forging ahead and leaving a track where the water has been disturbed. The implication seems to be that his dreams stirred up 'foul dust', which may be Nick's judgement on people like Daisy and Tom who 'smashed up things and creatures', but it certainly suggests the valley of ashes that represents the dark underside of the glittering world Tom and Daisy inhabit. The other meaning of 'wake', a watch beside a corpse, foreshadows the ending.

'…life is much more successfully looked at from a single window, after all.' (p.10)

2

⊣ This metaphor follows the paradox 'that most limited of all specialists, the "well-rounded man"'. By claiming that this is an epigram, Nick acknowledges that it was intended to be a clever, witty way of suggesting that people who are described as 'well-rounded' actually know very little about a lot of things. The metaphor suggests that, to be successful, you need to concentrate on one aspect of life, looking through a single window. This is also an interesting metaphor for Fitzgerald's narrative technique that employs a single narrator who is given only 'privileged glimpses' into other people's lives.

3 'I was within and without, simultaneously enchanted and repelled by the inexhaustible variety of life.' (p.37)

⬦ This quotation sums up the position of the partially involved narrator Fitzgerald has created. Although Nick is accepted by the communities he observes, he does not really belong, so he is paradoxically both 'within and without'. His ambivalent attitude to events, and particularly to Gatsby, is revealed in his admission that he is both 'enchanted and repelled'. This is particularly significant because it effectively describes Fitzgerald's own feelings about New York society in the Roaring Twenties.
(NB see **Contexts: Literary criticism: Psychoanalytic criticism** on pages 79–80.)

4 'On Sunday morning while church bells rang in the villages alongshore, the world and its mistress returned to Gatsby's house and twinkled hilariously on his lawn.' (p.60)

⬦ Fitzgerald specifically tells us that Gatsby celebrates the Sabbath Day with parties, suggesting that he seeks a mystical union, but not with God; he hopes his parties will bring him closer to Daisy. The misogyny of the narrator is revealed in the assumption that the world and everybody important in it is male. It is also significant that God is still worshipped in the villages alongshore, so, as far as Nick is concerned, the inhabitants of New York are 'The world', the only people who matter.
The connotations of the verb 'twinkle' are of something superficially bright, flickering intermittently, but insubstantial and ephemeral, like Christmas tree lights. By saying that the world 'twinkled' Fitzgerald exposes the emptiness of the lives of people for whom faith has been replaced by superficial hilarity.

5 '…I had no girl whose disembodied face floated along the dark cornices and blinding signs.' (p.78)

⬦ Fitzgerald has used the romantic image from the courtly love tradition of an unattainable woman to adore from afar. However, he has superimposed this spiritual 'disembodied face' on concrete references to the 'dark cornices and blinding signs' of New York City. The neon signs 'blind' the onlooker, suggesting not only the momentary glare of the bright lights but also, possibly, the way in which the signs blind the onlooker to the immorality of the activities they advertise.